THE TIDE TARRIETH NO MAN
1576

THE MALONE SOCIETY
REPRINTS, VOL. 179
2012

PUBLISHED FOR THE MALONE SOCIETY
BY MANCHESTER UNIVERSITY PRESS

Oxford Road, Manchester M13 9NR, UK
and Room 400, 175 Fifth Avenue, New York, NY 10010, USA
www.manchesteruniversitypress.co.uk

Distributed exclusively in the USA by
Palgrave, 175 Fifth Avenue, New York,
NY 10010, USA

Distributed exclusively in Canada by
UBC Press, University of British Columbia, 2029 West Mall,
Vancouver, BC, Canada V6T 1Z2

British Library Cataloguing-in-Publication Data
A catalogue record for this book is available from the British Library

Library of Congress Cataloging-in-Publication Data applied for

ISBN 978-0-7190-8931-2

Typeset by New Leaf Design, Scarborough, North Yorkshire

Printed by Berforts Information Press Ltd, Oxford

This edition of *The Tide Tarrieth No Man* was prepared by Peter Happé, and checked by H. R. Woudhuysen and G. R. Proudfoot. The Society is grateful to the Harry Ransom Humanities Resource Center at the University of Texas at Austin, Texas, for permission to reproduce their copy of the play (PFORZ 525 PFZ).

December 2011 H. R. Woudhuysen

INTRODUCTION

I

George Wapull's *The Tide Tarrieth no Man* was entered in the Register of the Stationers' Company on 22 October 1576:

xxij die Octobr' 1576 /
Hughe Iackson. / Receyved of him for his lycence to imprinte an Enterlude intituled
The tide tariethe noe man vj^{d}. & a copie[1]

As its title-page indicates, the play was printed by Hugh Jackson in 1576 at the sign of St John the Evangelist in Fleet Street.[2] Chronologically, the printing occurred at the beginning of Jackson's career which lasted from 1576 until 1616. Shortly after *Tide*, he printed two other surviving plays: the second known edition of the anonymous *King Darius* (1577), and Thomas Garter's *The Most Virtuous and Godly Susanna* (1578).[3]

Five complete copies of *Tide*, together with one fragment, have been collated for this edition:

British Library (C.34.f.45, cropped at top and side). This copy, with the acquisition stamp of 3 January 1856, is reproduced in *Early English Books Online*. [BL]
Folger Shakespeare Library (cs1548; perfect).[4] [FOL]
Huntington Library (69780, cropped at side).[5] [HN]

[1] W. W. Greg, *A Bibliography of the English Printed Drama to the Restoration*, 4 vols. (London, 1939–59), i. 5; Edward Arber, *A Transcript of the Registers of the Company of Stationers of London, 1554–1640 A.D.*, 5 vols. (London, 1875–94), ii. 303.

[2] A. W. Pollard and G. R. Redgrave, *A Short-Title Catalogue of Books Printed in England, Scotland and Ireland and of English Books Printed Abroad, 1475–1640*, 2nd edn., revised and enlarged by W. A. Jackson, F. S. Ferguson, and Katharine F. Pantzer, 3 vols. (London, 1976–91), no. 25018; Greg, *Bibliography*, no. 70.

[3] *STC* 6278 and 11632.5; Greg, *Bibliography*, no. 40(*b*) and no. 76.5. Some links between the printing of *Tide* and these plays are discussed below, p. xxi.

[4] This was the first of the two copies in the Mostyn sale at Sotheby's on 20 March 1919, lot 342; it went for £400 to G. D. Smith and was subsequently owned by John L. Clawson.

[5] This appears to be the copy bought by Richard Heber at Sotheby's in April 1821 for £22 1*s*. It was sold in the second part of his sale, 5 June 1834, lot 6410, for £52 10*s*. to the dealer Thomas Thorpe. It passed into the Devonshire collection.

Harry Ransom Center, University of Texas at Austin, Texas (PFORZ 525 PFZ; perfect).[6] This copy is the source for the present facsimile. [TEX]
Beinecke Library, Elizabethan Club, Yale (Eliz 240, cropped at side).[7] [Y]

The fragment is:

University Library Cambridge (Syn.7.57.38, consisting of sigs. E1 and the lower half of E2, containing TLN 1145–59 and 1181–95).[8] [CAM]

The following later editions have been consulted:

John Payne Collier (ed.), *The Tide Tarrieth No Man* (London, 1863), 1–82 (old spelling).[9]
Ernst Rühl (ed.), *Shakespeare Jahrbuch*, 43 (1907), 1–52 (old spelling).
John S. Farmer (ed.), *The Tide Tarrieth no Man* (London, 1910. Reissued New York, 1970) (facsimile of BL).
Edgar T. Schell and John D. Shuchter (eds.), *English Morality Plays and Moral Interludes* (New York and London, 1969), 309–66 (old spelling).

Very little is known for certain about the author, but it is possible that he is to be identified with the George Wapull who was the Clerk to the Stationers' Company from 29 September 1571 until 30 May 1575. Two entries in the Company's Register indicate his employment and salary:

to the Clarke for iij quarters wages viz from michelmas [29 September 1571] vntyll mydsomer 1572 xxx^{s}

[6] This was the second of the Mostyn copies, sold at Sotheby's on 20 March 1919, lot 343 for £440 to G. D. Smith. It was subsequently bought by Carl Howard Pforzheimer, see *The Carl H. Pforzheimer Library: English Literature 1475–1500*, 3 vols. (New York, 1940), ii. 534–5.

[7] Stephen Parks, *The Elizabethan Club of Yale University and Its Library* (New Haven, Conn., and London, 1986), p. 265; this copy, sold at Sotheby's on 27 June 1906, lot 963, for £176, was purchased by Quaritch; Alexander S. Cochran bought the copy from Quaritch and gave it to the Club in December 1911.

[8] This fragment was recovered from the binding of a copy of Humphrey Lynde, *Via devia* (London, 1630), *STC* 17095. The volume has a bookplate recording its presentation to Cambridge University Library by Bishop John Hacket in 1670.

[9] This inaccurate reprint was number 16 of Collier's Red Series and was included in the second volume of the collection *Illustrations of Early English Popular Literature*, 2 vols. (London, 1863–4); see Arthur Freeman and Janet Ing Freeman, *John Payne Collier: Scholarship and Forgery in the Nineteenth Century*, 2 vols. (New Haven, Conn., 2004), ii. 1261. Collier's activities are discussed below, pp. x–xi.

Among the charges for the period from 20 July 1572 to 20 July 1573 is:

Item paide to George Wapull Clearke for his yeres wages / due at midsommer laste [24 June 1573] xl^{s}[10]

The end of his appointment can apparently be determined from another entry:

Memorandum that I was sworne and admitted and Tooke charge of the clarkship of the Art or misterie of Stationers of the citye of London the xxxth of may 1575 *Anno xvij*^{o} *Regin*[a]*e Elizabeth*[*a*]*e* ... Richarde Collins.[11]

Mark Eccles notes that a George Waples was buried in St Gregory's, the parish church for the Stationers' Hall, on 9 October 1574. If this were the author it might account for both a posthumous printing of his work as well as the appointment of a successor. However, in February 1585, a George Wapull received ten shillings from the Company 'to further him in his voiage wch he p^{r}poseth into Norenbegue'.[12] This might have been the son of the Clerk. As Eccles opines, it is possible that either of these may have been the author, but he does not lose sight of the fact that it might have been neither.[13] Collier suggested that the spelling Wapull might be a variant form of Walpole.[14] It is possible that the *De pace inter Henricum Galliarum, et Eduardum Angliae, reges oratio* should be attributed to Wapull.[15]

The play's existence was known in succeeding centuries. Richard Rogers and William Ley referred to it as 'Tide tarries for no man' in their *Exact and*

[10] Arber, *Transcript*, i. 460, 465. [11] Ibid., ii. 35.

[12] W. W. Greg and E. Boswell (eds.), *Records of the Court of the Stationers' Company 1576 to 1602: From Register B* (London, 1930), p. 17; Arber, *Transcript*, i. 509. *Norembega* was a legendary settlement in North America, usually conceived of and mapped as being roughly in New England. Arber suggested that this entry might refer to Sir Walter Raleigh's second expedition to Virginia in April 1585, but Eccles notices that no reference to Wapull has been found in relation to it.

[13] See 'Brief Lives: Tudor and Stuart Authors', *Studies in Philology*, 79 (1982), Texts and Studies, no. 4, 124–5.

[14] Collier, *Tide*, p. ii. The two names seem to have mixed, but they probably derive from place names in Norfolk and Suffolk. Two marriages on Cornhill in London are close in date to the play: Hillary Wapolle married Joane Garret at St Peter's in 1557; and Roberte Kenigame married Alice Waullpoole at St Michael's in 1579: see C. W. Bardsley, *A Dictionary of English and Welsh Surnames* (London, 1901), pp. 792 and 791.

[15] (London, 1552), *STC* 1849. The author's name from the title-page and the dedication ascribes its authorship to 'Petrus Bello-Poelius Gallus', possibly a (challenging) Latinization of Wa[l]pull. The same person versified Franciscus Perussellus, *Summa christianae religionis* (London, 1551), *STC* 19783. However, 'Petrus' indicates someone called Peter rather than George; and 'Gallus' implies that this was a Frenchman.

perfect catologue of all playes that are printed (1656), and, in the same year, Edward Archer called it 'Tide tarrieth for no man', but did not supply an author's name. Francis Kirkman offered the play for sale in his *Catalogue* (1661), though he gave no detail other than the correct name of the playwright and the play.[16] A few years later, Gerard Langbaine, admitting that he did not know the play itself, mentioned it and its author, though he also erroneously gave the title as '*Tide tarrieth for no Man*'. As he provided details from the title-pages of other plays he had in stock and did not do so for this one, it seems possible that no copy was in fact available to him.[17]

The play continued to feature in eighteenth-century lists and catalogues of plays.[18] In David Erskine Baker's *The Companion to the Play-House* of 1764, the title is also erroneous, but its descriptive subtitle is given as '*A most pleasaunte and mery Comedie, ryght Pithy and fulle of Delighte*'. The entry includes the comment 'This Piece I never saw' and, like some other eighteenth-century descriptions, gives the play's date of publication as 1611 rather than 1576.[19] This raises the possibility that there may have been a reprint or a new edition, for, as noted above, Hugh Jackson did continue printing until 1616. In Isaac Reed's 1782 revision of *The Companion*, published as *Biographia Dramatica*, the date of 1611 is retained along with the comment about never having seen a copy; in addition to this, Hugh Jackson's entry for the play in the Stationers' Register is also given, but with the erroneous date of 26 October 1576.[20]

John Payne Collier reported in the 1863 preface to his edition of the play that he had bought a copy of it on behalf of the Duke of Devonshire 'about twenty years ago' and subsequently transcribed it for inclusion in the col-

[16] Greg, *Bibliography*, iii. 1326, 1337, 1351. The play is also referred to by Nicholas Cox in his *Exact catalogue* (Oxford, 1680), sig. B3^{r}.

[17] Gerard Langbaine, *An account of the English dramatick poets* (Oxford, 1691), sig. 2I6^{v}. He also refers to the play in *A new catalogue of English plays* (London, 1687), sig. E1^{v}, where he makes the same error in relation to the title.

[18] See, for example, those by William Mears, *A True and Exact Catalogue of All the Plays that were ever Yet Printed* (London, 1713), p. 42; Giles Jacob, *The Poetical Register*, 2 vols. (London, 1723), i. 300; William Rufus Chetwood, *The British Theatre* (Dublin, 1750), p. 37; Edward Capell, *Notitia Dramatica* (London, 1774), sig. g2^{v}; Joseph Ames, *Typographical Antiquities*, rev. William Herbert, 3 vols. (London, 1785–90), ii. 1134; and John Egerton, *Egerton's Theatrical Remembrancer* (London, 1788), p. 7.

[19] David Erskine Baker, *The Companion to the Play-House*, 2 vols. (London, 1764), i. sig. Y3^{r}; cf. ii. sig. 2H3^{v}. Other sources with the date 1611 include Jacob, Chetwood, and Capell.

[20] David Erskine Baker, *Biographia Dramatica, or, A Companion to the Playhouse*, rev. Isaac Reed, 2 vols. (London, 1782), ii. 372. It is not clear whether the reference to the Stationers' Register was taken from another printed source, or from the original manuscript of the Register. In the later edition of Baker's, *Biographia Dramatica*, rev. Isaac Reed and Stephen Jones, 3 vols. (London, 1812), iii. 337, the comment about not having seen a copy of the play has gone and its date of publication in black letter is given as 1576.

lection.[21] The purchase would thus have been made in about 1843. Collier's earliest account of the play is given at some length in the second volume of his *Extracts from the Registers of the Stationers' Company*, where he claimed it 'has never been noticed by any historian of our stage or poetry'.[22] In this account of the play he drew attention to what he called 'preaching' and to the activities of the Vice, as well as quoting the song which begins at TLN 1014. In the 1831 edition of *The History of English Dramatic Poetry*, Collier had made no mention of the play, but among his revisions for the 1879 edition of this work he inserted a passage which follows his 1849 account closely.[23] The new account of *Tide* comes after the original passage on *Nice Wanton*, but the list of plays in the chapter heading has not been changed to incorporate the new discovery.[24] Collier recorded that he knew of two copies, and, supposing that Wapull was a schoolmaster, he added the following intriguing detail:

> one of those [copies] bears strong evidence of having been much thumbed and read: certain marks upon it lead us to suppose that it had been actually a prompter's copy: the exits and entrances are marked in manuscript, and the names of Harris, Simons, and Charles are given as those of three of the performers, possibly boys in the author's school.

As nothing of this sort has been found on the copies consulted, this might suggest he saw one not now available, and it might corroborate the possibility of an untraced edition of 1611.[25]

[21] Collier, *Tide*, p. ii. The Devonshire copy is now in the Huntington, as noted above. Collier's autograph transcript is in the Folger Shakespeare Library (MS D.a.42). There is another transcript, owned in 1825 by W. S. Sloane, in the National Art Library of the Victoria and Albert Museum (Dyce MS 57). This may be the transcript sold in part 4 of the Heber sale, 8 December 1834, lot 2031. Another transcript owned by William Barnes Rhodes was sold by Sotheby's on 18 April 1825, lot 2557, for £2 12*s*. 6*d*. to Thorpe.

[22] John Payne Collier (ed.), *Extracts from the Registers of the Stationers' Company*, Shakespeare Society Publications, 38, 41 (1848–9), ii. 23–5. At the end of the second volume in the 'Report of the Council of the Shakespeare Society to the Eighth Annual Meeting of the Members' on 26 April 1849, p. 4, among 'works in the press, and in various stages of progress' is *Tide* to be edited from 'the unique copy ... in the library of the Duke of Devonshire'.

[23] John Payne Collier, *The History of English Dramatic Poetry*, new edn., 3 vols. (London, 1879), ii. 296–8. The play is incorrectly indexed as '*Time tarrieth no Man*' in 1879, and the entry is wrongly placed alphabetically, iii. 504.

[24] Compare the chapter heading in the 1831 edition, ii. 353 with the one in the 1879 edition, ii. 269. In the 1863 edition of the play, he indicates that he intended to follow the old spelling, but, whether deliberately or not, he introduced many differences which cannot be explained or relied upon.

[25] Collier, *History*, ii. 298. The addition of this passage about an unlocated prompt copy is not noticed by Freeman and Freeman, *John Payne Collier*, ii. 981–4, 1344–6, in their account of the 1879 edition of the *History*.

The play is a quarto in seven quires, collating A–G^4 and is signed on all rectos except for A, which signs only A2^r and A3^r.[26] Leaves are signed in the same form, with the exception of sig. B1 which appears as 'B.i.' rather than 'B.j.'. The title-page is framed with a border of printer's flowers and includes a doubling scheme: 'Fowre persons may easily play it' (TLN 7). This claim, as well as the description of the play as a 'commody, right pythie and full of delight' (4–5), are typical of the sales discourse used by printers of interludes at this period.[27] The title-page verso is blank. The Prologue, with a heading in large roman type (22), takes up sig. A2$^{r–v}$, concluding with 'Finis.' (79) and a design made up of printer's flowers smaller than those on the title-page. The text of the play starts on sig. A3^r with the initial stage direction for Courage's entry in the same large roman type (80). His first speech in dimeters is printed in double columns (81–131).[28] The play ends on G4^v with 'FINIS.' in small Roman type (1895), and a third set of printer's flowers.

The text, including the songs, is printed in black letter. Running titles, Latin quotations, stage directions, and speech prefixes are in roman type.[29] The running titles are normally 'A new Commody called' (verso) and 'The Tyde taryeth no Man.' (recto). They are printed in the same size of type as the heading for the Prologue, but some inconsistencies and variations in them are discussed below.

Speech prefixes are set in the left margin outside the body of the text.[30] As they are often out of line with the speeches to which they are meant to refer, it is likely that they were set as separate blocks of type of different size from the text in what is known as 'quotation quadrats'. This practice was difficult to manage and prone to error. It is noticeable that there are some individual pages where some of the prefixes are correctly aligned whilst others are not, as on C4^v (TLN 779), D3^r (931, 939, 952), and E4^r (1288), where the prefix is almost one line too high. In several places, there are irregularities

[26] The signature is lost together with some of the stage direction at the foot of sig. F2^r in BL.

[27] See Peter Happé, 'Printers of Interludes', in Kent Cartwright (ed.), *A Companion to Tudor Literature* (Chichester, 2010), pp. 192–210.

[28] Collier, *Tide*, prints these lines as six-line stanzas (sestets).

[29] Names of saints and authorities are treated inconsistently. The former are in roman type except 'Anne' (TLN 1225) and 'Paule' (1453, 1505). Most authorities and authors are in black letter, except Austen (45), Ambrosius (48), Socrates (594), Plautus (596), Periander (604), and Iuuenall (1095). 'Corage' (135) is in roman.

[30] In Y, speech prefixes on the rectos of sigs. D2, F3, F4, G4 are slightly obscured in the gutters because of the binding. The cropping at the side in BL, HN, and Y affects speech prefixes on versos, but not on rectos.

in the printing of the prefixes where the type has apparently moved.[31] For most pages the left-hand margin of the column for speech prefixes is strictly adhered to, but on B4^{r} and C1^{r} they are not all correctly left justified. The names of the characters in the prefixes are reduced to a single word, usually with a full stop, and a maximum length of 15 mm.[32] The following abbreviated forms are used: 'Further.' (Furtheraunce), 'Greedines' (without a stop; Greediness), 'Neighbor.' (Neighbourhood), 'Wanton.' (Wantonness), 'Wastful.' or 'Wastfull.' (Wastfulness), 'Christian.' (Christianity), 'Autho.' or 'Authori.' (Authority), 'Correcti.' (Correction).[33]

The text of each speech is preceded by a pilcrow (¶). The songs begin with a large Roman capital, but pilcrows are used before the first lines of second and later verses of each of the songs (TLN 273, 278, 283; 1024, 1029, 1034; 1339 1346). All the necessary catchwords are present, and they are usually accurate except for 'Wherby' instead of 'Whereby' (G1^{r-v}). They ignore speech prefixes, but they normally include the pilcrow, except that it is omitted on sigs. C3^{v} and F4^{v} and that it is erroneously added on E4^{v}. In all the copies the final letter of 'Then' on D2^{r} is distorted, perhaps caused by a damaged type or some debris. On A2^{v} the catchword is in the larger roman type of the following heading, preceded by the large printer's flower, known as 'vine leaf', as in the initial stage direction on A3^{r}.

There are a large number of stage directions. For the most part, entrances and exits are efficiently recorded. Usually entrances are centred on separate lines while exits are printed to the right, but not on separate lines. The exits are justified to the right edge of the measure, except for those at TLN 293, 530, and 1639 which are on the right but not justified, and, when space was tight, such directions were turned above or below the line (as at 659–60, 1699–1700, 1769–70, 1809–10). Both locations are used for directions about action, such as 'They both kneele, and Wastfull sayeth after Faythfull.' (centred at 1708), or 'Out quickly with his dagger.' (ranged right at 175). The word 'enter' is missing from the entry at 132; at 318–19, 'Greedines enter' is set in the left margin, and it looks as though this appears instead of a speech prefix. Exits are not marked for Furtheraunce (542), Tenaunt Tormented (820), Help, Profit, and Furtheraunce (1048), and Courage and Helpe (1354). 'Exiunt.' is wrongly used for exits of single characters (398,

[31] 'Corage.' (TLN 259), 'Helpe.' (290, 530), 'Courtyer.' (673), 'Corage.' (822), 'Wanton.' (883), 'Corage.' (1194), 'Helpe.' (1206), 'Wastful.' (1213), 'Wanton.' (1252), 'Greedines' (1564), 'Dispa ire.' (1690), 'Corage.' (1829). The speech prefix 'Wanton.' (1252) shows a development of space between 'o' and 'n': it is closed in BL, larger in HN, and largest in the other three copies.

[32] 'Faythfull.' usually has a stop, but the stop is absent at TLN 1823, 1842, 1862.

[33] 'Pro. Fur.' appears when two characters speak simultaneously at TLN 289.

777, 938, 1068, 1122, 1187, 1356, 1386, 1639, 1746, 1760); and on one occasion, 'Exit.' is used for two characters (1841).[34] 'Exiunt.' is misplaced at 1356, as it should cover the departure of Courage and Help at 1353. The pilcrow, which precedes the first word of the speeches, appears before stage directions at 132 and 498.

In quires A–E the normal practice for the centred stage directions, usually entrances, is to insert a blank line above and below the direction. The exceptions at TLN 132, 745, 749, and 1110, appear to have arisen because of pressure on space on those particular pages. For quires F and G, however, there are no such spaces for centred directions. Because the text neatly ends near to the foot of G4^{v} it is possible that this space-saving measure was adopted as a means of ensuring that the play was kept within the seven quires of paper. In this connection, it is notable that the play does not end with the woodcut portraying St John the Evangelist, the sign of Jackson's printing office, which appears in his other two extant plays discussed below.

None of the directions gives any indications about the layout of the stage or about stage furniture. Very few properties are mentioned, probably because the directions are concerned primarily with actions or movements, as with the two which mention the Vice's dagger (TLN 175, 1835). Many directions describe how the actors are to move about, especially in relation to one another: for example: 'Corage and Greedines enter as though they | saw not Christianity.' (1522–3). Some directions draw attention to physical appearance or costume on entry (TLN 567, 1436–9, 1664, 1686–7).

Two of the directions are of particular interest. One gives a useful hint about the nature of the copy used by the printer as well as an insight into stress on the doubling arrangements: 'And fighteth to prolong the time, while Wantonnesse | maketh her ready.' (TLN 1204–5). Such a direction is not likely to have been intended for 'literary' readers of the play: it must have been a note for the benefit of those engaged in performance, and thus it raises the likelihood that there was a direct relationship between an acting or prompt copy and the printed text. As far as the doubling arrangements are concerned, the direction 'Pause.' (1358) makes it look as though there had to be a short break while performers took time to get ready: once again, this would hardly be of interest to a 'literary' reader. The actor playing Courage has to change for the Debtor, and the one playing Wantonness, who may have been a boy performing the woman's part, has to change for the Sergeant.[35]

[34] These errors together with three errors in quotations (TLN 599, 1086, 1576) suggest that Latin was unfamiliar to the compositor.

[35] The term 'Pause' is sometimes used in other play texts to indicate a musical intervention: for consideration in French as well as Dutch contexts, see W. M. H. Hummelen, '*Pausa* and *Selete* in the *Bliscapen*', in Elsa Strietman and Peter Happé (eds.), *Urban Theatre in the Low Countries* (Turnhout, 2006), pp. 53–76.

This anxiety about a change of costume suggests that physical appearance and costume must have been thought important, as indeed is the reference to Despair's ugly shape (1686–7). It is apparent that the stage is cleared five times without continuity of action; thus extra time for changing roles and costumes might have been available at each of them as required.[36]

The soliloquies would have provided time for costume changes. However, reference to the doubling scheme in Appendix 2 shows that changes may sometimes have been allowed for by the skilful switching of actors. Thus Courage's twenty-line soliloquy at TLN 822–41 follows the exit of Player 1 as Tenant and precedes Player 4's entrance as Wantonness, neither of these two players coming under stress to make rapid costume changes. Similar switching is apparent for the soliloquies at 543–66 and 1123–6. On the other hand, Player 2 may have been less fortunate in having to hurry his change from Profit to Courtier during Courage's twenty lines at 1049–68. Player 4 was a little better off with 28 lines to change from Furtherance to Greediness at 680–707.

The detailed direction for an allegorical enactment (TLN 1436–9) is a notable feature near to the end of the play.

> Christianity must enter with a sword, with a title of pollicy, but
> on the other syde of the tytle, must be written gods word, al-
> so a Shield, wheron must be written riches, but on the
> other syde of the Shield must be Fayth.

The tapered form, a technical challenge to printers, is a typographical effect which could not be seen in performance, but this direction draws attention to the importance of the spectacular event which visually manifests the allegory. Subsequent directions give further details on how the allegory is to be developed (1502, 1886). It is not possible to be certain whether these varied directions are a record of what actually happened in performance, but if they are not, they suggest that someone thought very carefully about certain aspects of the forthcoming production. The absence of details about the stage itself, together with the inclusion of the doubling scheme, even though it is somewhat under pressure, may suggest that the play was designed for a small company of four who might perform almost anywhere, including the frequently used great halls of varying social status. No information has come to light about any specific performance of the play or about any location for it, though there are some references to parts of London as the action develops (St Paul's in 1164, 1166, 1395; Tyburn in 270, 1058, 1060; and the prison named the Counter in 1405).

[36] For the doubling scheme, see Appendix 2.

Examination of many commonplace minor flaws of type, spacing between letters, and evidence of the machining process, including some debris on the type face, indicates that all the six copies come from the same edition. The evidence of individual type and of the composition is supported by discernible similarities in the inking process during the machining which show the same letters are usually faint or partially printed in all the known copies. Debris in the form of what are probably hairs adhering to the type appears in all of them. These are visible in the facsimile.[37] Only one press variant has been found, and it seems that little attempt was made to proof copies during the printing process.[38] There are some minor differences between copies because of the shifting of type, but these appear to be accidental rather than deliberate, as for example 'wi ll' (TLN 437), 'th inke' (1210), 'Dispa ire.' (1690), and two probably related to one another 'Co urtyers' (617) and 'm oney' (618).

Evidence from spelling preferences gives no clear indication that more than one compositor was engaged on the volume. Some variant spellings which may indicate compositorial preferences are spread throughout, as in the fourteen instances of 'to' for 'too': 'too' does not appear. Similarly, the forms 'hither', 'hether', 'heather', 'hyther', 'thither', 'thether' occur throughout: both 'hether' and 'hyther' occur on sig. D4^v (TLN 1046, 1056). There is variation in words which in modern English begin with *en-* and *em-*: 'ingendreth', 'encourage', 'incorage', 'incouraged', 'incorager', 'intreate', 'imbrace', 'imbrase', 'imbraser'. The forms 'giue' and 'geue', as well as 'giues', 'giueth', and 'geues', occur irregularly, with both on sig. E3^r (1197, 1198) and 'giue' and 'geuen' on F4^r (1550, 1578). But there is perhaps some slight indication of a cluster of readings towards the end of the book. The form 'count' or 'counted' is favoured for most of the text until quire G where 'accoumpt' is preferred at 1667 and 1858 and 'acoumpted' at 1645 and 1648 (but there is 'coumpt' on sig. B1^r; 252, and 'accoumpt' on sig. C2^r; 604). 'Adew' and 'adew' appear seven times in quires B, C, and D, whilst 'Adue' and 'adue' appear six times after sig. D4^v (but 'adue' does appear with 'adew' on E2^v; 1161, 1187). However, these examples do not really make a convincing case for the work having involved more than one compositor, and such a view may be supported by the use of the 2-shaped *r* (ꝛ). Throughout the book, this letter occurs within words with great regularity after the letters *o* (most frequently), *b*, *d*, *h*, *p*, *w*, and *y*: it never occurs in the

[37] See 'money' (TLN 716), 'Marry' (1001), 'know' (1133), 'since' (1414), 'Greedinesse' (1774); see also 'hell' (127, left column).

[38] The variant at TLN 1531 is: nye,] TEX; nye. the rest. The distortion of the stop at the end of 1713 in BL and HN is discounted. At 801 the cramped comma before 'charge' may be a correction, but it is the same in all copies.

initial position. This practice is sustained when *-rr-* is required after any of these letters, with the 2-shaped *r* chosen systematically for the first of the pair.

To this may be added what appears to be a further inconsistency over upper-case initial letters for alliterated proper names such as Hurtful Help. On sigs. A3^{v} and B3^{v} there are instances where one word begins with a capital whilst its pair does not, as 'hurtefull Helpe' (TLN 145, 147), and 'no good Neighbourhood' (407, 410). On these two pages the same feature is found in the roman type used for the stage directions at 132 and 405.[39] These inconsistencies may be due to a need to compensate for a shortage of upper-case letters. In particular there seems to have been a shortage of upper-case 'F' in quires F and G for black letter and roman, as can be seen for 'Faithful Few': upper-case initial 'F' followed by lower-case initial 'f' appear in black letter at 1498, 1614, 1636, 1820 (at the start of a line), 1846, 1852 and in roman for the stage directions at 1468 and 1700, where the name begins the direction, and at 1786. At 1493 and 1877, both names begin with lower-case initial letters.

The usual page depth is 36 lines which is consistently adhered to. The exceptions are: C3^{r} (35 lines, perhaps to avoid starting a new speech at the foot of the page); C4^{v} (37 lines); D4^{r} (35 lines, because of the song, allowing verse two to begin at the head of D4^{v}); E4^{v} (34 lines, similarly, to allow verse one of the song to begin on F1^{r}); G4^{r} (35 lines); A2^{v} (26 lines of text, with spaces before and after verses and after 'Finis.', and the printer's flowers taking up space for about two lines of text); and G4^{v} (29 lines, with spaces before and after 'FINIS.', and the printer's flowers). Abbreviated and contracted forms are rare, with exceptions because of long lines in 'contēteth' (TLN 104, right column), 'beneuolēt' (1578), and '&' (1836). At 679 '&' (roman) appears twice in a long stage direction at the foot of the page. In the songs, the refrains are abbreviated by means of '&c.' (277, 282, 287; 1028, 1033, 1038; 1345, 1352). At TLN 1769, 'himselfe.' is turned up; and words are turned down at 480 'more.', 584 'fine.', and 1447 'blamed.'.

The text is carefully printed in terms of its generally tidy appearance and also the attention to detail.[40] Punctuation is managed effectively throughout, even though there are a considerable number of errors. On some occasions question marks are missing. In 47 places question marks have been identified as being used correctly and in 55 they are wanting. The most frequent absences are in quire E, but in this same quire there are 9 instances of correct

[39] It is a recurring feature that upper-case letters in the roman type for stage directions are often not fully inked or do not reach the paper completely, as at TLN 132, 498.

[40] No instances of turned letters have been found.

use.[41] However, the distribution of omitted marks is spread fairly evenly over the whole volume. One peculiarity is that the mark for a colon is very frequently preceded by a space, as for example 'ill :' (TLN 31) as distinct from 'place:' (52), both on sig. A2^r^. It is not clear whether such spaces were deliberately inserted or whether some individual pieces of type included them.[42] One idiosyncrasy which may be related to this is that (irregularly, but frequently) throughout the volume the compositor apparently inserted an extra space between words without any apparent cause. The first four instances are 'he is' (133), 'a Marchauntes' (179), 'a very' (202), and 'nor seekes' (286).[43] In the absence of corroborating evidence, and in view of its widespread occurrence, this phenomenon does not appear to point to there being more than one compositor.

Most lines are rhymed and end stopped; virtually every line ends with a punctuation mark. The compositor's eye for a tidy appearance complements the playwright's attention to tidy and regular versification. There are no lines divided between speakers, and where speeches are short they are rhymed into monometer or dimeter couplets, as at TLN 172–5. Most of the verse is in tetrameters, which means that few lines are too long for the measure.[44] Except in the Prologue and the songs, the compositor ignored the possibility of breaks after lines grouped in stanzas. These occasions are plentiful because of Wapull's extensive use of quatrains (rhyming aaaa and abab) and rhyme royal: he was an ambitious and versatile metricist, especially in the Vice's speeches.[45]

Four sets of headlines or running titles were in regular use. As noted above, the wording of the running title for each opening was meant to read 'A new Commody called' on the left page and 'The Tyde taryeth no Man.' on the right. For each of these there were two versions. The two 'Commody'

[41] Question marks are omitted or another mark is used at TLN 1263, 1273, 1275, 1277, 1279 on sig. E4^r^.

[42] Besides this frequently occurring anomaly for the spaced colon, there are a few instances where there is a space before a full stop, comma, and question mark, which may also have arisen because of the way the type was cast. D. F. McKenzie entertains but rejects the possibility of what he calls 'cast-on spaces' in his study of John Beaumont's *Psyche* which was printed by the Cambridge University Press in 1701–2, see 'Stretching a Point: Or, The Case of the Spaced-Out Comps', *Studies in Bibliography*, 37 (1984), 106–21.

[43] In quire D, for example, this feature is found at TLN 886, 900, 922, 925, 958, 971, 992. It appears to be distinct from spaces within individual words as at 617 and 618, where type may have slipped accidentally.

[44] Commas are inserted within some lines, though not all, and it seems likely that some of these were meant to mark caesuras, as for example in TLN 138–40, 145–7, 157–9, 163–4, 178–81. In some instances such commas interrupt the grammar in mid-line, as at 196–7, 240, 246, 260.

[45] See, for example, TLN, 680–707, 822–41; and Tenant in 779–820.

headlines can be separated into CA by the disparity in the height of the two letters 'll' in 'called', the first being taller than the second, and CB where these two letters are the same height. The 'Tyde' headlines are separable by the slightly raised 'o' in 'no', together with a more pointed tail for the first 't' in 'taryeth': these are named TA here. TB is identifiable by the absence of these features.

For the majority of quires, B–E, the following pattern is normal:

	recto	verso
1:	TA	CB
2:	TA	CB
3:	TB	CA
4:	TB	CA

In this part of the book, there is one variation in the composition of a headline. Another T form was set up with the spelling 'Tide' rather than 'Tyde'. This was used for B1^r instead of TA, as well as appearing on sig. A4^r.

For quires F and G the distribution of headlines is different. At the opening F3^v–F4^r, T and C are reversed; at G2^v–G3^r there are two instances of C and no T; and on G4^v there is T. On this last page of the volume, it may have been felt that a T headline on its own made better sense than a singleton C would have done. This being an outer forme, the two Ts had to be side-by-side for G1^r and G4^v, with the two Cs paired correspondingly for G2^v and G3^r. In the process of making this special arrangement, one of the T heads may have been damaged or distorted as the space between 'The' and 'Tyde' on G1^r is much greater than elsewhere.

The distribution for quires A, F, and G is:

A1^r	(tp)	F1^r	TA	G1^r	TB
A1^v	(blank)	F1^v	CA	G1^v	CB
A2^r	(Prol.)	F2^r	TA	G2^r	TB
A2^v	(Prol.)	F2^v	CA	G2^v	CB
A3^r	(Corage)	F3^r	TB	G3^r	CA
A3^v	CA	F3^v	TB	G3^v	CA
A4^r	T (Tide)	F4^r	CB	G4^r	TA
A4^v	CA	F4^v	CB	G4^v	TA

If F and G are rearranged by formes, the following shows how the headlines were manipulated:

Inner	F2^r	TA	F3^v	TB	G2^r	TB	G3^v	CA
	F1^v	CA	F4^r	CB	G1^v	CB	G4^r	TA
Outer	F4^v	CB	F1^r	TA	G4^v	TA	G1^r	TB
	F3^r	TB	F2^v	CA	G3^r	CA	G2^v	CB

In BL, TEX, and Y the same watermark appears in each of the seven quires, occurring across the fold once in each sheet, being roughly 70 mm by 20 mm. It depicts a hand, with the wrist and part of the palm on one side of the gutter, while the fingers and thumb, which point to a five-pointed flower or star, appear on the other. The watermark corresponds roughly to nos. 10868–81, 11138, 11189, 11248 in Briquet's *Filigranes*, and thus the paper may have originated in central or south-west France.[46] The following distribution of these marks has been observed:

BL		TEX		Y	
A2	fingers	A2	palm	A2	palm
A3	palm	A3	fingers	A3	fingers
B1	fingers	B2	palm	B1	fingers
B4	palm	B3	fingers	B4	palm
C2	fingers	C2	fingers	C2	palm
C3	palm	C3	palm	C3	fingers
D1	fingers	D1	fingers	D1	fingers
D4	palm	D4	palm	D4	[not available]
E1	palm	E2	fingers	E2	palm
E4	fingers	E3	palm	E3	fingers
F2	palm	F2	palm	F2	fingers
F3	fingers	F3	fingers	F3	palm
G1	palm	G1	palm	G2	[not available]
G4	fingers	G4	fingers	G3	fingers

The palm of the hand tends to be obscured in the gutter because of the binding. However, in some quires of TEX there are a '3' and the initials 'RP' on the palm.

In none of the quires for which data is discernible does the same pattern appear throughout, with the possible exception of quire D. This means that the half of the sheet containing the marks was sometimes laid at one end of the tympan and sometimes at the other. However, there does seem to have been some change in the paper supply, as all the watermarks in the Huntington copy show grapes and a pot with the initials RG. This may suggest that the amount of paper stock for each quire was set aside before machining and that the HN stock was towards the bottom of each pile. Another possible explanation is that there was a small sub-issue on better-quality paper.

[46] Charles-Moïse Briquet, *Les Filigranes: dictionnaire historique des marques du papier dès leur apparition vers 1282 jusqu'en 1600*, ed. Allan Stevenson, 4 vols. (Amsterdam, 1968).

Of the two plays printed by Jackson shortly after *Tide*, the printing of *Susanna* shows more similarities with *Tide* than does *Darius*. The layout of the title-pages is similar in that *Susanna* uses the same pattern for the border on the two sides and the head of the page. The border at the foot is thinner, perhaps because there was more information to be included, especially as the doubling scheme for eight players had to be longer. Though choices of individual fount are different line by line, there is a noticeable similarity in the layout and in the way the varieties of type—black letter, roman, italic—are made to set off one another. In contrast, the choices of fount for *Darius* are more limited, almost all the title-page being in black letter. Though it is claimed that six persons may easily perform this play, there is no scheme showing the division of the parts.

Within the main texts there are also notable similarities between *Susanna* and *Tide*. Both separate the speech prefixes into a dedicated column of type, abbreviating them where necessary to keep within this measure. Each marks the beginning of speeches with a pilcrow which is justified to the left of the main body of the text. Stage directions are usually centred and sometimes tapered. The practice of inserting line spaces before and after centred stage directions is generally followed in *Susanna*, but the spaces are eliminated when there is pressure on space, as they are in *Tide*. The visual effect is similar, with plenty of blank space to the right and the speech prefixes neatly regulated to the left. When the Vice speaks in dimeters, both texts print the short lines in two columns (*Susanna*, sigs. $B4^{v}$–$C1^{r}$, $C2^{v}$, $D3^{r-v}$, $D4^{r}$ [wrongly signed B4], $E4^{r}$, $E4^{v}$).

In *Darius* speech prefixes are centred, and a different version of the pilcrow is used at the beginning of the speeches. This arrangement implies a less economical use of paper since each speech prefix requires its own line. There are fewer variations of type, the stage directions and the running titles being in black letter like the text, without variation of size.[47] Nor does the compositor resort to double columns.

The implications are that the printing of *Tide* and *Susanna* were similarly conceived. Whether the same compositor was at work must remain an open question, but there were clearly similar intentions over a range of production decisions. In contrast, the arrangements for *Darius* seem to have been thought out quite differently, even though it comes from the same printing office, and it was apparently printed chronologically between the other two. The explanation of the difference may be that Jackson's edition of *Darius* is a page-for-page reprint of Thomas Colwell's edition of 1565.

[47] In both these volumes the running titles are the same for rectos and versos. The difficulty in the last quire of *Tide* over separate heads does not therefore arise.

II

No source for the play's plot has been found. The sequence of events involves demonstrations of the culpable activities of the Vice and his associates, and much of the play's dynamic revolves around these rather conventional actions. The dramatist is much exercised to cite the eponymous proverb as frequently as possible by characters good and bad.[48] The plot itself involves the prompting of Greediness, the principal character, to satisfy his evil and destructive impulses, which in the end lead to his own destruction. Other characters are introduced as victims of Greediness and of the Vice and his fellow conspirators. Such a plot, which is largely episodic, is hardly dependent upon a source so much as a series of theatrical conventions. However, there is marked interest in the use or application of proverbial and wise sayings, and these are almost always attributed to classical or theological authors.

The appearance of *Tide* in 1576 can be seen in several different contexts. These include theatrical and literary conventions and the closely linked topics of theology and economics. The conventions are interesting because of the creation of a number of interludes which are designed in similar ways with similar conventions in mind. This relationship extends to subject matter as well as to a remarkable number of performance characteristics. It is apparent that there were several playwrights working in London at this time whose assumptions about the nature of drama and also about what might be undertaken in relation to social concerns were remarkably alike.

Though Avarice, one of the seven deadly sins, had been a lively player in the drama from *The Castle of Perseverance* in the fourteenth century, it is a remarkable feature of the early years of the reign of Queen Elizabeth I that wealth and its abuses became the focus of some writers of interludes. Growing prosperity was accompanied by the accumulation of riches and, at the same time, this aroused social concerns about those who did not benefit from the success of economic enterprise and were indeed victims of it. The plays mostly to be associated with *Tide* in this respect are *Wealth and Health* (1557),[49] *The Longer thou Livest the More Fool thou Art* (William Wager, 1559–68), *The Cruel Debtor* (1560–5), *The Contention between Liberality and Prodigality* (1567–8), *The Trial of Treasure* (?William Wager, 1567), *Enough is as Good as a Feast* (William Wager, *c.*1570), and *All for Money* (Thomas

[48] With slight variations in the wording, the proverb appears 20 times in the text: TLN 39, 64, 70, *86* (left column), *119* (right column), *146*, *382*, *454*, *522*, *630*, 744, 806, *839*, *889*, *900*, 1104, 1185, *1263*, 1680, 1732. Of these, 11 are spoken by the Vice (italicised here). Usually the citation of the proverb is signalled in the text by an initial capital letter for 'Tide'.

[49] This play may be Marian in origin, being entered in the Stationers' Register in August/September 1557.

Lupton, 1577).[50] In all likelihood these plays were written with London in mind and, like *Tide*, they often refer to specific places there.

This group of plays, remarkable for their appearance within a few years of one another, has several features in common, suggesting a prevalent appetite and concern. The authors shared a sense of the possibilities of vigorous stage presentation. The Vice in the forms of Ill Wit (*Wealth*), Inclination (*Trial*), Covetous (*Enough*), Sin (*Money*), as well as Courage (*Tide*), triumphs as a central dramatic feature, together with the mischief associated by this period with his activities and those linked to him. Onstage events like the bridling and unbridling of Inclination in *Trial* and the vomiting by Money in *Money*, which acts as a kind of birthing for his son Pleasure and his grandson Sin, argue a developed sense of what could be good spectacle but also morally illuminating. The plays share a topical sense of economic and social ills, including fraud, rationalizing the profit motive, the prevalence of the corruption of justice and the oppression of the poor, and evils such as poverty, excessive rents, and the exploitation of the predicament of debtors. Treasure is associated with pleasure and Fortune in *Liberality* and *Longer*, and *Trial* illustrates the vanity of material pleasures in general. Two notable interpretative aspects are found in several of them. One is that wealth may have good outcomes if properly used, an idea which might have been very acceptable to those who had it among successful London merchants. The other is that some of the plays are Calvinist in tone, as in the promotion of the doctrine of the elect in *Enough* and *Trial*.[51]

The economic aspects and their abuses were considered in part in theological terms, and *Tide*, like other plays in this group, reflects some of the issues of the Elizabethan religious settlement. The play shows both exploiters and victims, and the dynamics of the plot are arranged to reveal how the fates of both are developed. Wapull, like some of his contemporaries, saw the picture of economic ills as linked with the spiritual fate of the characters. His targets include usury, bribery, extortionate interest on loans, excessive rents, and false dealing between borrowers, in addition to the petty crimes of cutting and stealing purses. The principal exploiter in *Tide* is Greediness, who is also called Wealthiness.[52] This is not so much an alias

[50] Most of these 'wealth' interludes are considered by Paul Whitfield White, 'Interludes, Economics, and the Elizabethan Stage', in Mike Pincombe and Cathy Shrank (eds.), *The Oxford Handbook of Tudor Literature, 1485–1603* (Oxford, 2009), pp. 555–70, and Peter Happé, 'Wealth in the Interludes', *Cahiers Elisabéthains*, 77 (2010), 1–8. See also Ineke Murakami, 'Wager's Drama of Conscience, Convention, and State Constitution', *Studies in English Literature*, 47 (2007), 305–29.

[51] For fuller details of plots, characters and themes, see Darryll Grantley, *English Dramatic Interludes 1300–1580: A Reference Guide* (Cambridge, 2004).

[52] There is a character called 'Greedigut' in *The Trial of Treasure*.

as a way of setting up two contrasting reactions to his activities. On his first entry he shows himself troubled in his conscience having encountered a preacher who attacked 'greedy guttes' and 'euell members of a common welth' (TLN 332, 333). Courage, named as the Vice on the play's title-page, immediately cites the eponymous proverb and urges him to make the most of his opportunity to create riches. In spite of the ambiguous nature of wealth, a theme which is sustained in other wealth interludes, and his elaborate protests about being both good and bad (93–110, right column), this Vice makes his evil intentions plain to the audience unashamedly. He expresses satisfaction at having suppressed Greediness's conscience and at having encouraged him to avoid virtuous inclinations and to follow the devil (401–4). Greediness's subsequent activities show him exploiting Willing to Win Worship, who is dressed as a courtier, by making him loans at a time opportune to them both and then causing distress by heavy interest and taking excessive profits. He also shows himself dominated by the Vice's promotion of the proverb, which encourages him to take the plunge and make the most of financial opportunity.[53] Noticing that other courtiers need loans, Greediness sets off to St Paul's Cross where he intends further to disregard the preachers to be found there and to take the opportunity of seizing debtors. The wider significance of this proposal has a social implication since this episode is dependent upon courtiers' need to raise money in order to take part in the process of making a good show before their Prince. This theme is repeated elsewhere in the play (TLN 583), and, by relating greed to the court's proceedings, the play adopts a stance critical of the court's financial practices. Later, another Debtor is arrested by the Sergeant and complains that Greediness will not allow him enough time to pay off his debt (TLN 1388–1401). This episode also involves an unsuccessful attempt to extort a bribe by the Sergeant.

Another economic aspect is touched upon by Hurtful Help. He is a broker who gains advantage by apparently bringing benefits which are later shown to be false. He reveals that he loves best to deal with foreigners at the French or Dutch churches in London where the merchants are willing to outbid the English (TLN 477–9). This chauvinistic association with foreigners who are too powerful is presumably a reference to a popular prejudice.

The passage concerning Greediness's seizing of opportunity turns upon time's crucial role in the play, a factor which is inherent in its proverbial title.[54] Here there is a special significance in the word 'tide'. Tilley's citation

[53] At one point this Vice says 'hap good or ill' (TLN 628), a notion which may have been suggested by the attitude to taking a chance by Haphazard, the Vice in R. B.'s *Apius and Virginia*, printed the year before *Tide*. See the soliloquy at sig. B3^{r-v}.

[54] It is notable that two other plays in the wealth group have proverbs for titles.

for the proverb is 'Time and tide (The tide) tarries (stays for) no man', with the earliest example in *Everyman*.[55] However, it may be even earlier as B. J. Whiting cites Chaucer.[56] In its entry for the noun 'tide' the *Oxford English Dictionary* separates six main meanings concerned with time and a further eight such meanings concerned with the tide of the sea.[57] The entry concludes that the word originally meant 'time' from *Beowulf* onwards (?eighth century AD), but that in the sixteenth century it was more generally used with reference to the sea. Here, in the play, this latter meaning may indeed be in mind as it is evident that the opportunities, which the Vice encourages his victims to seize, do go out like the sea. In his appropriation of the proverb, it has been suggested that the Vice actually distorts it. The proverb is meant to advise one to make good, indeed virtuous, use of time while it lasts, but his intention is clearly to the contrary, a prompt towards *carpe diem*.[58] This contrariness is a theme of his first soliloquy where he explains his ambiguous nature:

> Corage contagious,
> When I am outragious,
> In working of yll:
> And Corage contrary,
> When that I doe vary,
> To compasse my will. (TLN 87–92, right column)

In the context of the Barge in his opening soliloquy, he refers specifically to 'high tyde' (84, left column) and 'ebbing and flowing' (126, right column).[59] But, in the play's didactic mode, it is clear that time can be the opportunity for good outcomes as well as bad ones. If the creation of wealth does indeed depend in part upon time, so does the opportunity of salvation, provided that it too is taken at the right time (808).

In this connection, the stage is cleared about half way through the play for a key speech at a pivotal moment by the Tenant who is a second victim of 'that cruell tyger, my Landlord Greedinesse' (TLN 787). He has held his tenancy for forty years and he is now aged and thrust out from his home.

[55] Morris P. Tilley, *A Dictionary of the Proverbs in England in the Sixteenth and Seventeenth Centuries* (Ann Arbor, Mich., 1950), T323. In Clifford Davidson, Martin W. Walsh, and Ton J. Broos (eds.), *Everyman and Its Dutch Original, Elckerlijc* (Kalamazoo, Mich., 2007), pp. 24–5, it is apparent that this proverb at l. 143 was an addition to the Dutch original by the English adaptor.

[56] Bartlett Jere Whiting, *Proverbs, Sentences, and Proverbial Phrases from English Writings Mainly Before 1500* (Cambridge, Mass., and London, 1968), T318.

[57] *OED* tide *n.* I.1–6 and II.7–14.

[58] Robert Weimann and Douglas Bruster, *Shakespeare and the Power of Performance: Stage and Page in the Elizabethan Theatre* (Cambridge, 2008), p. 31.

[59] A 'boate straight into hell' is envisaged by the Vice at TLN 1773.

His neighbour, No Good Neighbourhood, one covetous of his property, has enlisted Greediness's help to eject him. Tenant has grasped that this is all the result of 'following the instructions, of cursed Corage' (813) in accordance with the proverb quoted here once more. But rather than live by thievery (804), he will seek a remedy by finding true Christianity, thus providing an entry for the author's spiritual concerns. Tenant does not reappear in the action, perhaps because of the exigencies of the doubling scheme, but his intention to find a spiritual solution is carried forward in the allegory of Christianity developed in the play's second half. He makes a specific link to this reforming aspect of the proverb by his reference to 'the tyde of Gods mercy and grace' (808), a point which is anticipated in the Prologue (67). For the moment, he imagines that Christianity is bound or dead, lying in the dust (817).

The allegory concerning the role of Christianity is dramatically conceived. It has already been noticed that his entry is envisaged in symbolic detail; the following episodes are designed to present a visual demonstration of the dramatic action's significance. The allegory's focal point is the sword and shield carried by Christianity, the accoutrements themselves reminiscent of St Paul's armour.[60] As the allegory's narrative develops, the sword's title or inscription opposes 'pollicy' with 'gods word', and the shield contrasts 'riches' and 'Fayth' (stage direction at TLN 1436–9). The word 'pollicy' has significance at this time, partly because it is often associated with the Vice, but also here the implication is that the government, or those wielding economic power, operate in a ruthless and unscrupulous way, or perhaps a combination of both, and are acting against God's word. The hints about the Prince and the courtiers are pertinent at this point, as indeed is the reaction against the activities of foreigners who are allowed to benefit economically at the expense of the indigenous population. The naming of 'gods word' and the title 'Fayth' on the shield are both characteristic of the language of the Protestants. Indeed, the two terms presumably refer to central Protestant doctrines in the emphasis upon the power of scripture (*sola scriptura*), as well as the primacy of faith (*sola fides*).

A further twist is added to the allegory by naming the character who turns the titles round and thus signifies reformation as Faithful Few. This identification inclines the play's religious stance towards Calvinism and the doctrine of the elect. Such an affinity may be further supported by the Calvinistic notion of the divine calling to one's appropriate place in the community which should not be challenged.[61] In the process of reforming Christianity, Faithful Few attacks Greediness. He discovers that Christianity, now

[60] St Paul's armour is specifically mentioned at TLN 1453.
[61] White, 'Interludes, Economics, and the Elizabethan Stage', p. 556.

in a deformed state, had to yield to the 'greedy great' (TLN 1509), calls Greediness a 'Christyan with a canckered heart' (1554), and comments that 'Usury is a science and art' (1649). His words of reproach are apparently effective, even though Greediness chooses riches and policy rather than the alternatives. There is a remarkable irony here, for Greediness does finally succumb to a figure who is a preacher in spite of his earlier contempt for one. It is reported that in a state of madness and despair he kills himself and is carried off to hell in a boat reminiscent of the one Courage had mentioned at the play's beginning. Thus the ending brought in by Authority, involving the purifying of Christianity, is seen as having heavy and fateful consequences. As is the case with the death of Worldly Man in Wager's *Enough is as Good as a Feast*, death and damnation are part of the assertion of doctrine and of underlying moral issues and matters of belief.[62]

The Vice's adherence to and exploitation of the proverb in the title lead to his intervention in another incident. This hinges in part upon the misuse of wealth, as the plot is concerned with the marriage between Wastefulness and Wantonness, a young woman eager for the physical and worldly indulgence of married life. Courage advises her to defy her mother and to marry young, taking the opportunity of doing so as the proverb prompts. He persuades the couple to continue in their way of life, and their acceptance of his persuasion is expressed in the song about pleasure which they sing with him. Once the marriage has taken place, the newly-weds quarrel over the consumption of their wealth and over the husband's need to acquire more profit in order to fund their extravagant and careless life. In the end, they separate and Wastefulness is threatened by Despair, who in this case makes a stage appearance 'in some ougly shape' (TLN 1686). But Faithful Few brings out in Wastefulness an awareness of 'Gods mercifull promises' (1737), another characteristically Protestant phrase. By acknowledging these, Wastefulness is able to escape and to hurry off to 'reforme' his wife (1742). Thus the issues relating to wealth are to be met by means of spiritual awareness rather than by a practical sense of how to solve economic problems. The spiritual element is underlined by one sinister intervention by Courage. After approving the action of Fained Furtherance, a Merchant's man, who has exploited the old Tenant and his persecutor No Good Neighbour by gaining profit from both of them, he offers a heretical idea. Courage claims that 'soule there is none, when the body is dead' and that 'after this life, there is nothing but blisse. | There is no soule, any payne to abide' (TLN 561, 564–5).

The Christian teaching in the play has a humanist context in as much as Wapull makes reference to a number of authorities. These are most likely reflections of works encountered in the education system of the time, and they

[62] Ibid., p. 564.

are complementary to the Christian interpretation of the eponymous proverb. They include references to Greek figures: Socrates (TLN 594, 1854), Periander (604), Antisthenes (1577), Pythagoras (1587), Aristotle (1594, 1630), Plato (1655), as well as Latin authors: Sallust (371), Plautus (596), Juvenal (1095), and Seneca (1657). The Christian authors are Augustine (45), Ambrose (48), Hyemes (392),[63] and Paul (1453, 1505).

The presence of the doubling scheme and the frequency of stage directions point to the play's theatrical potential. In this respect, Wapull shows a lively appreciation of possibilities. That he should do so is remarkable in that he is not the only writer of interludes who adeptly manages and indeed exploits the necessity of doubling even though his experience of playwriting was apparently limited. It is a feature of the 'wealth' group of interludes that they show an awareness of staging possibilities. Most of them have doubling schemes which suggest that they were written with small companies in mind. Though the possibility of amateur performance in educational establishments should not be ruled out, it seems that these writers were aiming at quasi-professional production. That would involve a commercial undertaking by a company deriving some income from performance, even though its members may not have made their living solely from work as actors. As it happens, the publication of *Tide* occurred in the same year as the opening of James Burbage's Theatre which brought about a change in the commercial management of the acting profession.

As the doubling chart in Appendix 2 shows, Wapull exercises the four actors to the limit, there being several occasions in the play when all four are on stage together. Doubling also taxes the actors' versatility because of the variety of roles each must play. It has been pointed out that the reappearance of the actors disguised, but also detectable, in sharply contrasted roles may have added to the audience's appreciation of the entertainment.[64] Indeed, the onlookers may well have been expecting that such enjoyable changes might take place. Another significant feature is the process by which the characters address the audience directly: in this play the stage is cleared on six occasions to allow this to happen.[65]

The play's staging potentialities are underlined by the stage directions. Courage is a comprehensive example of the Vice in that he exhibits attributes of this dominating role which had become well established by the time the

[63] See the note to this line in Appendix 1.

[64] David Mann, *The Elizabethan Player: Contemporary Stage Representation* (London, 1991), pp. 24–6.

[65] Bernard Beckerman, 'Playing the Crowd: Structure and Soliloquy in *Tide Tarrieth No Man*', in J. C. Gray (ed.), *Mirror up to Shakespeare: Essays in Honour of G. R. Hibbard* (Toronto, 1984), pp. 128–37.

play was written. He is on the stage continuously for large sections of the play; the actor playing the part is required by the doubling scheme to undertake only the very brief role of the Debtor (TLN 1387–1435). At one point, as the stage direction at TLN 1769–70 indicates, he adopts two contrasting voices while he conducts a dialogue with himself. He has ten soliloquies in which he takes the audience into his confidence and shamelessly reveals the ambiguities which mask his evil intentions.[66] This self-revelation, in a mode typical of the Vice, shows his characterisation to be a metatheatrical function rather than one based upon psychological realism. He is supported by a group of villains whose names he helps to make look innocuous (136–66). He weeps conspicuously over the death of Greediness, which he has helped to bring about (stage direction at 1761), and carries a dagger which he is quick to use even against his allies whom he calls his 'schollers' (776; stage directions at 175, 1835). The Vice's enquiry about whether Help likes this 'play' (1203) may be about clever and improvised sword play which fills up the time required for the costume change.[67] He sings in three songs which celebrate the success of his activities, the first two with his group of conspirators Profit, Help, and Furtherance (266–88, 1013–39) and the third with Wantonness and Wastefulness, two of his victims, assisted by Help (1330–52).[68] At one point he has a substantial passage of contradictory nonsense of the 'I was very sore hurt, but I have not a wound' type (294–317).[69] In the end, he is justly punished by Authority and sent to gaol, but characteristically he wriggles to the last, inviting someone with a curst wife—a member of the audience perhaps—to escape from her by taking his place (1838–9). In short, his performance is marked by the combination of moral wickedness and theatrical versatility which is characteristic of the role at this period.

*

[66] TLN 81–131 (left and right columns), 294–317, 399–404, 543–66, 680–707, 822–41, 939–50, 1049–68, 1123–6, 1762–85. At one point he directly addresses the women in the audience, TLN 700.

[67] Possibly the Vice's verbal play on clapping (TLN 1056–60) is accompanied by improvised physical activity as he 'claps' his Cousin Cutpurse whether in real or mimed action.

[68] These are the only songs in the play and they all have four singers, the entire company in varying roles. Wantonness, the only female character, who might be expected to be played by a boy, is doubled with male characters, including Greediness and Authority.

[69] This type of nonsense still appears today in performances of revived folk plays and in some nursery rhymes ('I went to the pictures tomorrow | I took a front seat at the back'). See 'Tangletalk' in Iona and Peter Opie, *The Lore and Language of Schoolchildren* (Oxford, 1959), pp. 24–6.

The editor is grateful for valuable help from: the staff of the Rare Books Room, Cambridge University Library; Ryan Hildebrand, Book Cataloguing Department, Harry Ransom Center, University of Texas at Austin; Stephen Tabor, Curator of Early Printed Books, at the Huntington Library, San Marino, California; and Stephen R. Young, Beinecke Rare Book and Manuscript Library, Yale University.

The present edition is a 1:1 photofacsimile text of the Harry Ransom Humanities Resource Center at the University of Texas at Austin, Texas, copy of the play. The play has been provided with Through Line Numbers (TLN), beginning with the title-page.

There are a few readings which, although decipherable in other copies of the quarto, may be unclear in the photofacsimile of the Texas copy. In these transcriptions, except for punctuation, italic is generally used for roman and roman for black letter:

Sig. A3^{v} TLN 134–52

Profyte. ¶I tould thee that heare we should him not misse.
Helpe. ¶Good mayster *Corage* most hartely good euen. *Salute corage*
Corage. ¶In fayth my friendes welcome, all three by saynt *Steuen.*
Iesus good Lord how doe ye fare?
Couer your heads,why are you bare?
And how syrs,now syrs, leade you your liues,
Which of all you three ,now the best thriues?
Helpe. ¶Tush man none of vs can doe amisse,
For we doe alwayes take time while time is.
And where euer we goe like counsayle we giue,
Telling all men that here they shall not still liue.
Corage. ¶Therein hurtefull Helpe, thou doste very well,
The Tyde taryeth no man,thou must alwayes tell.
Helpe. ¶Indeede hurtefull Helpe, that is my name,
But I would not that all men should know the same.
For I am a broker the truth is so,
Wherefore if men in me hurtfulnesse should know,
There are few or none that with me would deale,
Therefore this word hurtfull I neuer reueale.

Sig. B2^{r} TLN 313–17

I was very sore hurt,but I had not a wound.
I buskeled my selfe as though fight I would,
And tooke me to my legges as fast as I could.
And so with much payne hither I did come,
But husht syrs I say,no moe wordes but mum.

Sig. B4r TLN 436–41

Neighbor. ¶I thanke you syr euen with all my harte,
And I trust also that Helpe will doe his parte.
Helpe. ¶Doubt not but that I to thee will be cleauing,
Therefore proceede and shew him thy meaning.
Neighbor. ¶Then syr this is the matter, if it shall please you giue eare,
I haue a neighbour who dwelleth to me somewhat neare.

Sig. B4v TLN 482–503

Therefore though thou be straunge,the matter is not great,
For thy money is English,which must worke the feate.
Neighbor. ¶In deede my money as a neighbour will agree,
With any man wheresoeuer it be.
And I my selfe would be a neighbour to,
And therefore the rather I doe that I doe,
For if it were not to be a neighbour by them,
I wisse I would not take a house so nye them.
Helpe. ¶I dare say ech man would be glad at his harte,
To haue all his neighboures such as thou arte.
What matter is it,if thou thy selfe be sped,
Though thou take thy neighbours house ouer his head.
Corage. ¶Tush that is no harme,but rather it is good,
For he doth it only for pure neighbourhood.
See yonder commeth one,if thou canst make him thy friend,
Then mayest thou shortly bring thy purpose to end.

¶*Furtheraunce entereth*

Further. ¶Now Mayster Corage how doe you fare.
Corage. ¶Euen glad to see that you so merry are:
Furtheraunce you must pleasure a friend of myne.
Further. ¶Thereto I am ready at ech tide and tyme,
To doe for him what in me doth lye.

Sig. D1r TLN 793–806

What neighbourhood is, may also be seene,
My neighbour supposed,is my deadly foe :
What cruell chaunce,like to mine hath beene,
Both my house and liuing,I must now forgoe.
What neighbour is he,that hath serued me so?
Thus crewelly to take my house,ouer my head,
Wherein these forty yeares,I haue bene harbored and fed.
And now being aged,must thus be thrust out,
With mine impotent wife,charge,and famely :

Now how I shall liue, I stand in great dout,
Leading and ending,my life in misery.
But better doe so,then as they liue, by theeuery,
Catching and snatching,all that euer they can,
Because that(say they)Tyde taryeth no Man.

Sig. D1^{v} TLN 830–41

The virgins which are but tender of age,
Rather then their trim attyre should swage.
Their tayles for new they will lay to gage,
To euery slaue,peasaunt,and page.
The graund signyoures,which in yeares are rype,
With couetous clawes,like the greedy grype.
Their pore brethren, from their liuinges do wype,
And euermore daunce,after Corages pype.
Corage neuer in quiet doth lye,
But the Tyde taryeth no man, still he doth crye.
Therefore worke thy will by and by,
That rich thou mayest be,when euer thou dy.

Sig. G3^{v} TLN 1811–18

Authori. ¶Vpon thy selfe,iust iudgement thou doest giue,
Iuuenall sayeth, Citties are well gouerned,
Whereas such rebelles are now suffered to liue,
But after their desertes,are iustly punished.
Corage. ¶They which are Rebelles,it behoooueth in deede,
That they be corrected and punished so,
For they doe much harme in euery steede,
But I am none such,I would you should know.

Sig. G4^{r} TLN 1836–9

Correcti. ¶In fayth sir, now I wil geue you the check, *& catcheth him*
Corage. ¶Oh gods passyon, wilt thou breake my neck?
Is there no man here that hath a curst wife,
If he will in my stead, he shall end his life.

TLN 1863–6

Great tranquillity to vs shall befall :
We shalbe a ioy to ech godly nation,
When Christianity is deliuered from thrall.
For better it were vnchristened to be,

Sig. G4^{v} 1883–6

Faythfull. ¶God graunt that so it may be kept,
As all Christians it may become :
And for my part it shall not be slept,
But my duty shall straight way be done. *he turneth the titles*

APPENDIX 1

NOTES ON ERRORS AND DOUBTFUL READINGS

Suggested corrected readings are in parentheses.

26 with *(*which*)*

73 acte *(*ade, *Collier, mistaking the damaged, ligatured* ct *type for* d*; cf.* effect *TLN 602)*

84 (right column) which that *(*that which*)*

132 *(lacks* Enter*)*
Hurting *(*Hurtfull*)*

219 agayne *(?*agaynes*)*

236 sight *(?*fight*)*

299 steale *(probably acceptable: cf. OED steal sb[1] 4a, a handle; this would fit conj. Schell and Shuchter in next)*
scumber *(*scummer *conj. Schell and Shuchter; but perhaps scumber, dung of dog or fox (OED) should be read here, to rhyme with* number *TLN 298 even though the first citation is 1655)*

302 [2]brother *(In* TEX o *is damaged making it similar to* e. *The other copies unmistakably have* o, *but there is some damage to this letter in Y)*

318 *(Lacks a speech prefix for Greediness)*

392 Hyemes *(*James *[New Testament author] conj. Schell and Shuchter, possibly referring to James 5:1–6)*

599 pepereris *(*peperceris, *Plautus, Aulalaria II.8.10)*

734 growte

918 an *(*on*)*

1086 non tarit *(*nuntiaret *conj. Schell and Shuchter)*

1125 alone *(?*done*)*

1202 heate *(?*beate*)*

1356 Exiunt *(see Introduction, p. xiv)*

1473 were *(*we're*;* we were *conj. Schell and Shuchter)*

1479 man *(?*men*)*

1497 [2]me *(?*thee*)*

1576 audire cum besecerint *(*audiri cum bene fecerunt *conj. Schell and Shuchter)*

1609 it *(*it is*)*

1725 thrall *(*woe *To rhyme with* know *TLN 1723: conj. Collier)*

1756 see *(?*be*)*

1856 or *(?*of*)*

1885 slept *(*slipped *conj. Schell and Shuchter)*

APPENDIX 2

DOUBLING SCHEME

On the play's title-page the order of appearance of characters for each player is correct, except that Player 4 plays Despair before he plays Authority.

Player	1	2	3	4
22–79	Prologue			
80			Courage	
132	Help	Profit	Courage	Further.
294			Courage	
318			Courage	Greed.
399			Courage	
405	Help	Neigh.	Courage	
498	Help	Neigh.	Courage	Further.
531			Courage	Further.
543			Courage	
567		Courtier	Courage	
644	Help	Courtier	Courage	Further.
680			Courage	
708			Courage	Greed.
745		Profit	Courage	Greed.
774–7			Courage	
778–820	Tenant			
821			Courage	
842			Courage	Wanton.
939			Courage	
951	Help		Courage	
978	Help	Profit	Courage	Further.
1049–68			Courage	
1069		Courtier		
1105		Courtier	Courage	
1123			Courage	
1127	Help		Courage	Greed.
1188	Help		Courage	
1212	Help	Wasteful.	Courage	
1239	Help	Wasteful.	Courage	Wanton.
1355		Wasteful.		Wanton.
1359–86		Wasteful.		

Player	1	2	3	4
1387–1435			Debtor	Sergeant
1436		Christian.		
1468	Faithful	Christian.		
1522	Faithful	Christian.	Courage	Greed.
1624	Faithful	Christian.		
1640	Faithful			
1664	Faithful	Wasteful.		
1686	Faithful	Wasteful.		Despair
1719	Faithful	Wasteful.		
1747–60	Faithful			
1761			Courage	
1786	Faithful		Courage	Authority
1824	Faithful	Correction	Courage	Authority
1842	Faithful			Authority
1872–94	Faithful	Christian.		Authority

THE Tyde taryeth no Man.

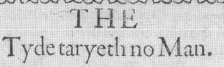

A MOSTE PLEA-ſant and merry commody, right pythie and full of delight.

Compiled by George Wapull.

¶ Fowre perſons may eaſily play it.

1. The Prologue, Hurtfull help, the Tenaunt, Faithfull few for one.
2. Paynted profyte, No good Neighbourhood, the Courtyer, Waſtefulneſſe, Chriſtianitye, Correction for another.
3. Corage the Vice, Debtor, for another.
4. Fayned furtheraunce, Grœdineſſe the Marchaunt, Wantonneſſe the Woman, the Serjaunt, Authority and Diſpayre, for another.

¶ *Imprinted at London, in Fleete-*
ſtreate, beneath the Conduite, at the
Signe of Saynt Iohn Euaungeliſt,
by Hugh Iackſon.
1576.

THE
Tyde taryeth no Man.

A MOSTE PLEASANT
and merry commody, right pythie and full of delight.

Compiled by George Wapull.

¶ Fowre persons may easily playe it.

1. The Prologue, Hurtfull help, the Tennaunt, Faithfull few, for one.
2. Paynted profite, No good neighbourhood, the Courtier, Wastefulnes, Christianitye, Correction, for another.
3. Corage the Vice, Debtor, for another.
4. Fayned furtheraunce, Greedinesse the Marchaunt, Willfull wanton the woman, the Sergeaunt, Authority and Dispayre, for another.

¶ Imprinted at London, in Fleetestreete, beneath the Conduite, at the Signe of Saynt Iohn Euangelist, by Hugh Iackson.
1576.

The Prologue.

AS the worme which in the timber is bred,
The selfe same timber doth consume and eate:
And as the moth which is commonly fed,
In the cloth with her bred, and the same doth frete.
So many persons are a damage great,
To their own countrey, which hath them relieued,
And by them their own countrey ofte times is greeued.

¶So many citties and townes are defamed,
By reason that some inhabitauntes is ill:
So that for ones facte, the whole towne is blamed,
Although the residue to good doe their will.
Yet the fact of this one, the others good name doth spill,
And thus a reproch to his own towne ingendreth,
And the good name of the whole town he hindereth.

¶To what ende these wordes we haue spoken,
In our matter shalbe more playnely exprest,
Which the Tide tarieth no man, to name hath token,
For that it is moste agreable and best.
Because that no man from his pleasure will rest,
But ech man doth take the time of his gayne,
Although the same be to others great payne.

¶For so greedy is the person auaricious,
Whome Saint Austen doth well liken to hell,
For that they both are so much insacious,
That neyther of them know when they are well.
And Ambrosius doth verify and tell,
How that couetous persons do lack that they haue,
And therefore not satisfyed till they are in graue.

¶But where such people are, small loue there doth rest,
But greedy desyre supplieth the place:
The symple ones commonly, by such are opprest,
For they nothing way, any needy mans case.

A.ij. But

But with greedy grype, their gayne they imbrace,
No kind of degree that they will forbeare,
Neyther any time they will let slip or spare.

¶ And although that here a Courtyer is named,
Yet thereby is not ment the Courtyer alone:
But all kindes of persons, who their suites haue framed,
Or to any such greedy guttes, haue made their mone.
Being driuen to their shiftes, to haue ought by lone,
How greedinesse at such times, doth get what he can,
And therefore still cryeth, Tyde tarieth no man.

¶ Which prouerbe right well might be applyed,
To a better sence then it is vsed:
There is time to aske grace, this may not be denyed,
Of thy sinfull life so greatly abused.
Let not that time then be refused,
For that tyde most certayne will tarry no man,
Thus taking the prouerbe, we rightly do scan.

¶ Thus worshipfull Audyence, our Authour desyreth,
That this his acte you will not depraue:
But if any fault be, he humbly requireth,
That due intelligence thereof he may haue,
Committing himselfe to your discretions graue,
And thus his Prologue he rudely doth end,
For at hand to approche, the Players intend.

Finis.

Courage

Courage the Vice entreth.

To the Barge to,
Come they that will go,
Why sirs I say whan:
It is high tyde,
We may not abide,
Tide taryeth no man.
If ye will not go,
Why then tell me so,
Or else come away straight:
If you come not soone,
You shall haue no roome,
For we haue almost our frayte
There are Usurers great,
Who their braynes doe beat,
In deuising of guyles:
False dealers also,
A thousand and mo,
Which know store of wyles.
Crafty cutpurses,
Maydens mylchnurses,
Wiues of the stampe:
Who loue mo then one,
For lying alone,
Is yll for the crampe.
Husbandes as good,
As wigges made of wood:
We haue there also,
With seruauntes so sure,
As packthred most pure,
Which men away thro.
There are such a sight,
I cannot resite,
The halfe that we haue:
And I of this Barge,
Haue the greatest charge,
Their liues for to saue.

Corage contagious,
Or courage contrarious,
That is my name:
To which that I will,
My mind to fulfill,
My maners I frame.
Corage contagious,
When I am outragious,
In working of yll:
And Corage contrary,
When that I doe vary,
To compasse my will.
For as in the Bee,
For certayne we see,
Sweete honey and sting:
So I in my mind,
The better to blind,
Two corages bring.
And as with the sowre,
Ech day and hower,
The Phisition inuenteth:
To mingle as meete,
Something that is sweete,
Which his pacient contēteth.
Euen so some while,
To collour my guile,
Do geue corage to good:
For I by that meane,
Will conuey very cleare,
And not be vnderstood.
Now syr to showe,
Whether we do goe,
Will doe very well,
We meane to preuayle,
And therefore we sayle,
To the Diuell of hell.

A.iij. And

And though it be farre,
Yet welcome we are,
When thether we come:
No chere there is,
Whereof we shall misse,
But be sure of some.
I Corage do call,
Both great and small,
To the Barge of sinne:
Wherein they doe wallow,
Tyll hell doe them swallow,
That is all they do win.
When come ye away,
Thus still I doe say,
As lowde as I can:

Take time while time is,
Least that you doe misse,
Tyde taryeth no man.
With catching and snatching
Waking and watching,
Running and ryding:
Let no time escape,
That for you doth make,
For Tyde hath no byding.
But ebbing and flowing,
Comming and going,
It neuer doth rest:
Therefore when you may,
Make no delay,
For that is the best.

¶ Hurting helpe, Paynted profite, Fayned furtheraunce.

Helpe. ¶ By the masse syrs see where he is.
Profyte, ¶ I tould thee that heare we should him not misse.
Helpe, ¶ God mayster Corage most hartely good euen. Salute corage
Corage. ¶ In fayth my friendes welcome, all three by saynt Steuen.
Jesus good Lord how doe ye fare?
Couer your heads, why are you bare?
And how syrs, how syrs, leade you your liues,
Which of all you three, now the best thriues?
Helpe. ¶ Tush man none of us can doe amisse,
For we doe alwayes take time while time is:
And where euer we goe like counsayle we giue,
Telling all men that here they shall not still liue.
Corage. ¶ Therein hurtefull Helpe, thou doest very well,
The Tyde tarieth no man, thou must alwayes tell.
Helpe. ¶ Indeede hurtefull Helpe, that is my name,
But I would not that all men should know the same,
For I am a broker the truth is so,
Wherefore if men in me hurtfulnesse should know,
There are few or none that with me would deale,
Therefore this word hurtfull I neuer reueale.

My

My name I say, playne Helpe to be,
Wherefore ech man for helpe doth come vnto me.
Good mayster Helpe, helpe to that or this,
And of good reward you shall not misse.

Profite. ¶And as thou from Helpe, hurtfull doste throw,
So paynted, from Profyte, I must forgoe,
For if any man know me, for profyte but paynted,
Men will but little with me be acquaynted.
My mayster who a good gentleman is,
Thinketh me as profitable as he can wish.
So that playne Profite, he thinketh my name,
And before his face, my deedes shew the same.

Further. ¶Farewell my maysters for I may hence walke,
For I see you two will haue all the talke.

Fayne a going out.

Corage. ¶What fayned Furtheraunce are you so coy,
Will you neuer leaue the trickes of a boy,
Come agayne I say, least I doe you fet,
And say what thou wilt, here shall no man let.

Further. ¶Fet mee?

Corage. ¶Yea fet thee.

Further. ¶Marry doe what thou dare.

Corage. ¶That will I not spare. Out quickly with his dagger.

Helpe. ¶Good syr hold your hand, and beare with his rudenesse,

Corage. ¶Nay I cannot nor will not suffer his Lewdenesse.

Further. ¶Tush a figge for him, let him doe what he can.

Corage. ¶Alas syr who are you, but a Marchauntes man,
Good syr what you are, we know right well,
Who is your mayster, and where you doe dwell,
You professe that your mayster you doe greatly further,
And yet for his goodes, you would him gladly murther.

Further. ¶If so I doe wish, it is long of thee,
For thou therevnto haste encouraged mee.

Profyte. ¶What husht I say, no more of these wordes,
For appeaching oft, the appeacher disturbes.

We

Be friendes agayne as you were at the firſt,
Let ech man ſay the beſt, and leaue out the worſt.
Further. ¶ I for my part doe therevnto conſent. And ſhake handes.
Corage. ¶ Then geue me thy hand if thou be content.
Now are we friendes, as at firſt we were,
Therfore ſtraight way thy mind let vs here.
Further. ¶ Truely I meane to doe euen as doe the reſt,
For in mine opinion that is the beſt,
And as hurting helpe, hath hurting forgone,
And paynted profyte, is profyte alone,
So I fayned furtheraunce, henceforth doe minde,
To be furtheraunce playne, leauing fayned behind:
Other mens furtheraunce to ſeeke I will ſay,
Yet will I ſeeke mine owne as much as I may.
Corage. ¶ Elſe werte thou vnwiſe, yea and a very foole,
Thou learnedſt none otherwiſe, I trow in my ſchoole.
I am a ſchoolemayſter for you three moſt fytte,
Who indued you with courage, in ſtead of great wytte.
Helpe. ¶ To be our mayſter wilt thou take in hand,
Why we are as good as thou, thou ſhalt vnderſtand.
Corage. ¶ Alas pore knaues, what could you three doe,
If you haue not courage belonging thereto.
Helpe. ¶ And what can courage doe without helpe,
As much as a kitling or ſuckling whelpe.
Corage. ¶ And by hurtfull helpe, what am I the better,
Being holpe to a hurt, I am no great getter.
Helpe. ¶ It is folly with thee thus to contend,
We are as good as thou, and ſo I doe ende.
Corage. ¶ Since that by wordes I can no mayſtry haue,
I would proue what my manhood wyll doe ſyr knaue.
Profite. ¶ Why arte thou blind, mayeſt thou not ſee,
That agayne thee one, we are here three.
Corage. ¶ And what can three doe agaynſt one,
I hauing courage, and they hauing none.
Therefore courage will claw you or you goe hence,
Now defend your ſelues I will ſee your fence.

¶ What

Helpe. ¶What Corage I say thy hand now stay.
Corage. ¶Will you then consent to that which I say.
Helpe. ¶There is no remedy but we must consent,
Sometimes it is good a fooles minde to content:
Therefore I am content to be thine inferiour,
And I will from henceforth take thee for superiour.
Corage. ¶And so will the residue I trow also.
Profyte, ¶If you say I syr, we will not say no.
Corage. ¶Well syrs, then I will shew you my minde,
But fyrst I will discribe you, ech one in his kinde.
Thou helpe arte a broker, betweene man and man.
Whereby much deceyte thou vsest now and than,
Profite is one, who by seruice in sight,
Doth cause his mayster to thinke him most right.
A profytable seruaunt, he thinketh him to be,
Because he is profytable, while he doth him see.
And fayned Furtheraunce, doth fayne him to further,
His mayster and others, whome fayne he would murther.
Thus in seeking welth you all doe agree,
And yet you professe others friendes for to bee.
Profite. ¶Ne quisque sapit, qui sibi non sapit,
This saying I redde, when as I went to schoole,
One not wise for himselfe, is but a very foole.
Helpe, ¶By my troth, and of that opinyon am I,
And in that opinyon I meane for to dye.
Further. ¶Tush why spend you tyme in speaking of that,
While thereon you talke, in vayne is your chat.
For who helpes not himselfe, before any other,
I coumpt him a foole, if he were my brother.
And as I count him, all people doe so,
Therefore cease this talke, and hence let vs go.
For some of vs may chaunce to meete with a chiding,
Because that so long from home we are biding.
Profyte. ¶By S. Anne I thinke therein thou say well,
For I know thereof I am like to here tell.
Corage. ¶Why man a little while breaketh no square.

B.i. ¶Tush

Helpe. ¶ Tush helpe hath excuse, to colour that care.
Further. ¶ Yea but already we haue tarryed to long.
Helpe. ¶ Why then ye were best goe without a song.
Further. ¶ Nay I will tarry to sing, though therefore I should dye.
Profite. ¶ My helpe to singing, I did neuer denye.
Corage. ¶ Why then syrs haue at it coragiously.

The Song.

Fyrst Corage causeth mindes of men,
to wish for good or ill:
And some by Corage now and then,
at Tiborne make their will.
Helpe, Profite, and Furtheraunce do fayne,
Where Corage doth catch in any mans brayne.

¶ Then helpe in hope to haue his pray,
full secretly doth wayte:
And as the time doth serue alway,
he throweth forth his bayte.
Helpe, Profite, &c.

¶ Profite prolongeth not the time,
to please his paynted mind:
He passeth not though mayster pyne,
so he his pleasure find.
Helpe, Profite, &c.

¶ And Furtheraunce, thou last of all,
he came into the rowte:
He wayeth not his maysters thrall,
nor seekes to helpe him out.
Helpe, Profite, &c.

Finis.

Pro. Fur. ¶ Now Corage farewell for we must be gone.
Help. ¶ Nay syrs you two shall not go alone.

For

For I doe meane to beare you company,
And so shall we be euen a whole trinity.
Therefore Corage adewe. They three go out.

Corage. ¶ Syr here was a trinity in a witnesse,
A man might haue shapte three knaues by their likenesse.
A trinity much like to the trinity of late,
Where good wife Gull, brake her goodmans pate.
In came her man to make vp the number,
Who had his nose shode, with the steale of a scumber.
But in fyne, these three began to agree,
And knit them selues vp in one trinity.
And after they loued like brother and brether,
For very loue, they did kill one another.
And then they were buried, I doe well remember,
In Stawtons strawne hat, vij. mile from December.
Where they had not lyen the space of a day,
But fower of those three, were thence run away.
The Constable came, with a backe on his bill,
And because they were gone, he did them kill.
I Corage so cleft their Cushions a sunder,
To see how they bled, it made me to wonder.
I my selfe was smitten twise to the ground,
I was very sore hurt, but I had not a wound.
I buskeled my selfe as though fight I would,
And toke me to my legges as fast as I could,
And so with much payne hither I did come,
But husht syrs I say, no moe wordes but mum.

Greedines enter. ¶ Tushe talke not of that, for in vayne you doe prate,
For there are none but fooles, that welthines doe hate.

Corage. ¶ What Greedinesse I say, why what is the matter,
Mayster welthinesse I would say, whereon doe you clatter?

Greedines ¶ What old friend Corage, arte thou so nere hand,
Marry I will shew thee, how the matter doth stand.
As I walked along, through by the streete,
By such wayes as mine affayres did lie:
It was my chaunce with a preacher to meete,

B.ij. Whose

Whose company to haue I did not deny,
And as we two together did walke,
Amongest other communication we had,
The Preacher brake out with reprocheable talke:
Saying that we cittizens were all to bad,
Some of vs he sayeth are gréedy guttes all:
And euell members of a common welth,
He sayeth we care not whome we bring to thrall,
Neyther haue we regard vnto our soules health,
His talke I confesse my conscience did nip,
Wherefore no longer I would him abide,
But sodenly I gaue him the slip,
And crossed the way to the other syde.
So alone I let mayster Preacher walke,
And here by chaunce I stombled in.

Corage. ¶ And arte thou so foolish for any such talke,
To cease or stay thy welth for to win.

Greedines ¶ Serra, he cried out of excessiue gayne,
Saying when any of our wares haue néede,
Then doe we hoyst them vp to their payne,
And commonly make them pay for their spéede.

Corage. ¶ I perceiue that fellow was hote of the spirite,
He would not haue you take time while time is,
If ye follow his councell, he will begger you quite,
But what aunswere diddest thou geue him to this?

Greedines ¶ Why thou knowest my quallity is such,
That by contrary talke, I vse no man to blame,
For although often my doinges they touch,
Yet my talke alwayes to the tyme I frame.
When he sayd excessiue gayners were ill,
I sayd for them it was a shame,
And in all thinges else, I pleased his will:
And so I fayned my selfe without blame.

Corage. ¶ Thou doste wisely therein, I commend thée therefore,
For what euer thou thinke, yet say as they doe,
So shalte thou haue their fauoures euermore,

And

And that way no blame thou shalt come vnto.

Greedines ¶ Yea but truely his wordes did my conscience prick,
Of me he did so vnhappely gesse,
I promise thee he touched me vnto the quick,
For that in gayning I vsed excesse.
My conscience doth tell me, I haue done amisse,
And of long time I haue gone astray,
And a thousand witnesses the conscience is,
As Salust in moste playne wordes doth say.

Corage. ¶ Why doltish patch, arte thou so vnwise,
To quayle for the saying of such a knaue,
Thou knowest all the world will thee despyse,
And a begging thou mayst goe, if that naught thou haue.
And how shalt thou haue ought,
If thy gayne be not great:
Consider this well in thy minde,
Remember thy house, and thy wife that peate,
Must still be kept in their costly kinde:
Therefore take the time, while the time doth serue,
Tyde taryeth no man, this thou doste know,
If thy goods decay, then mayst thou sterue,
So doing thou seekest thine own ouerthrow.

Greedines ¶ In deede as thou sayest, it doth me behooue,
Not so rashly to lay my gayning aside,
Least so my selfe a foole I doe proue,
By shooting from my profyte so wyde:
I consider my welth is now at good stay,
Which I would be loth should be impared,
For once rich, and after in decay,
Is a miserable thing, as Hyemes hath declared.
Therefore I meane thy councell to take,
Least of that misery I know the smart,
Then is it to late any mone to make,
Or from such foolishnesse to reuart.
Therefore Corage adew vnto thee,
For it behooueth me hence to departe. Exiunt.

B.iij. ¶ Adew

Corage. ¶Adew Welthineſſe till agayne we ſee,
Adew great greedineſſe with all my hart,
Hath not Corage contagious now ſhewd his kinde,
By encouraging Greedineſſe vnto euill:
Which late was drawing to a better minde,
And now agayne doth follow the Deuill.

Enter Helpe, and no good Neighbourhood.

Helpe. ¶Loe thee Neighbourhood, where Corage doth ſtand.
Corage. ¶What no good Neighbourhood, geue me thy hand.
Neighbor. ¶Thoſe two fyrſt ſyllables, might be put out,
And then thou hitteſt my name without doubt.
Corage. ¶Why is not no good Neighbourhood thy name?
Neighbor. ¶Put away no good, and ſee how it will frame.
For if thou doe put away no good,
There reſteth no more but neighborhood.
Corage. ¶Then is it neighbourhood, neither good nor bad,
Nay though we leaue the fyrſt, it is good the next we had.
For leauing out no, put good to the reſt,
Then is it good neighbourhood, thus I thinke is beſt.
Neighbor. ¶Nay I will haue them both two left out,
Becauſe of my name men ſhould ſtand in doubt:
For if no good neighbourhood I be named,
Then of all men I ſhall be blamed.
And if that good, to neighbourhood I haue,
Men will ſay I doe it prayſe to craue.
So I will leaue out both no and good,
And will be indifferent ſole Neighbourhood.
Corage. ¶Then Neighborhood be it, if ſo it ſhall be,
And neighborhod, what is thine errand to me?
Neighbor. ¶Syr my comming, is for occaſions two,
The fyrſt is for your councell, what were beſt to doe,
In a matter which I haue lately begon,
If I ſhall procede, or elſe leaue it vndone.
The ſecond is, if I ſhall procede,

That you will ſtand my friend if I neede.
Corage. ¶ Aſſure thy ſelfe thereof without doubt,
Therefore ſhewe thus the matter thou goeſt about.
Neighbor. ¶ I thanke you ſyr euen with all my harte,
And I truſt alſo that Helpe will doe his parte.
Helpe. ¶ Doubt not but that I to thee will be cleauing,
Therefore proceede and ſhew him thy meaning.
Neighbor. ¶ Then ſyr this is the matter, if it ſhall pleaſe you giue eare,
I haue a neighbour who dwelleth to me ſomewhat neare,
Who hath a Tenement, commodyous and feate,
To which Tenement I beare a loue very greate.
This man my neighbour as far as I can learne,
Hath in his Tenement but a ſhort tearme,
Fower or fyue yeares or there about,
Which tearme you know, will ſoone be worne out.
Now ſyr might I in reuerſion, a leaſe thereof haue,
I would giue the Landlord, euen what he would craue.
Corage. ¶ And who is the Landlord, thereof can you tell?
Neighbor. ¶ Mayſter Greedineſſe, a man whome you know right well,
He is one which neuer did mony hate.
Corage. ¶ Why then ſpeake in time, leaſt thou be to late,
The Tyde taryeth no man the prouerbe hath ſayde,
Therefore ſee no time herein be delayde,
Mayſter Helpe here ſhalbe to thee a ſtay,
For with mayſter greedineſſe, he beareth great ſway.
Helpe. ¶ I will doe for him what lyeth in me.
Neighbor. ¶ And then to your paynes I will gladly ſee.
Corage. ¶ Doubt not then, but thou ſhalt haue thy mind.
Neighbor. ¶ As you ſay, I wiſh that I may it find,
But I doubt that of my purpoſe I ſhall miſſe,
By reaſon of one thing, and that is this:
My foreſayd neighbour which now holdeth the ſame,
Hath bene there a long dweller of good name and fame.
And well he is beloued both of yong and old,
Wherefore not onely the neighbours with him will holde.
But alſo the Landlord, I am in great doubt,

B.iij. Wilbe

Wilbe therefore vnwilling to put him out,
And I but a straunger among them God wote.

Helpe. ¶ Marry syr it is much the better for that,
For if thou werte more straunge, and borne out of the land.
Thou shouldest sooner haue it I dare take in hand,
For among vs now, such is our countrey zeale,
That we loue best with straungers to deale,
To sell a lease deare, whosoeuer that will,
At the french, or dutch Church let him set vp his bill.
And he shall haue chapmen, I warrant you good store,
Looke what an English man bids, they will giue as much (more.
We brokers of straungers, well know the gayne,
By them we haue good rewardes for our payne.
Therefore though thou be straunge, the matter is not great,
For thy money is English, which must worke the feate.

Neighbor. ¶ In deede my money as a neighbour will agree,
With any man wheresoeuer it be.
And I my selfe would be a neighbour to,
And therefore the rather I doe that I doe,
For if it were not to be a neighbour by them,
I wisse I would not take a house so nye them.

Helpe. ¶ I dare say ech man would be glad at his harte,
To haue all his neighboures such as thou arte.
What matter is it, if thou thy selfe be sped,
Though thou doe take thy neighboures house ouer his head.

Corage. ¶ Tush that is no harme, but rather it is good,
For he doth it only for pure neighbourhood.
See yonder commeth one, if thou canst make him thy friend,
Then mayest thou shortly bring thy purpose to end.

¶ Furtheraunce entereth

Further. ¶ Now Mayster Corage how doe you fare.

Corage. ¶ Euen glad to see that you so merry are:
Furtheraunce you must pleasure a friend of myne.

Further. ¶ Whereto I am ready at ech tide and tyme,
To doe for him what in me doth lye.

Therefore

Therefore let me know your mind by and by.

Corage. ¶Serra, of thy mayster a lease he would haue,
And therein thy friendship it is, he doth craue.

Neighbor. ¶Syr, if that herein my friend you will stand,
I will giue you therefore euen what you will demaund.

Further. ¶Then Neighbourhod thou shalt shortly see,
That I can doe somewhat betweene my mayster and thee.
Thou couldest neuer speake better to speede,
For of money now he standeth in neede.
To pay for a purchase of certayne land,
Which needes he must discharge out of hand.
Therefore this time for thee well doth fall,
If that thou haue money to tempt him withall.

Neighbor, ¶Tush man for money I will not spare,

Further. ¶Then needest thou no whit for to care,
And if thou take payne now to walke home,
There shalt thou fynd him sitting alone.

Corage. ¶Cocks passion man hye thee away,
Thou knowest the Tyde for no man will stay.

Neighbor. ¶Why syr but will you not walke with vs thither?

Further. ¶No, doe Helpe and you goe before together,
And I warrant you I will not long be behind you,
For though I be absent, yet I will mind you.

Neighbor. ¶Then syr adew till we meete agayne,
Doubt not but I will consider your payne.
Come Helpe shall we goe.

Helpe. ¶It is time I trow. Exiunt.

Further. ¶Ah syr this geare doth trimly fall out,
I know this lease, which he goeth about:
Wherefore I will worke so on both the sydes,
That of both parties I will obtayne brybes,
I will shew the old Tenaunt how one goeth about,
To take his house and to thrust him out.
Wherefore he will largely grease me in the hand,
Because his friend therein I shall stand.
The other here did promise me playne,

C.j. That

That he would reward me for my payne.
Therefore Corage farewell vnto thee,
For how this geare will frame, I will see.

Corage. ¶ Farewell Furtheraunce, my gentle friend,
A man may seeke Hell, and such two not find.
I meane a friend, so worthy to trust,
And a neighbour, that is so honest and iust.
Of honesty I trow, he is meetely well sped,
That will take his neighbours house ouer his hed.
I thinke there is no man, within this place,
But he would gladly such neighboures imbrace.
Where two such neighboures dye out of one towne,
The Deuill shall be sure, to haue one black Gowne.
As well he is worthy, if I might be iudge,
For in their affayres, he dayly doth trudge.
Good councell he giues them, both morning and euening,
What meanes they shal worke, to their neighbors greeuing.
He teacheth them how, to pill and to poule,
In hope after death, to haue body and soule.
Tush what meane I thus, of soule for to speake,
In vayne with such talke, my braynes I doe breake.
For soule there is none, when the body is dead,
In such kinde of doctryne, my schollers I leade.
Therefore say I, take time, while time is,
For after this life, there is nothing but blisse.
There is no soule, any payne to abide,
The Teachers contrary, from truth are far wide.

Willing to win worship, enter Courtyer like.

Courtyer. ¶ Oh so my hart is filled with doubt,
Which way I may worke, my worship to win:
Shall I leaue of Courtyers, so iolly a rout,
And eke of Ladies a company so trim.
And shall I home to my cottage rude,
There to liue like a countrey clowne:

Truely

Truely I know not which way to conclude,
To get my selfe worship and renowne.
To win worship I would be right glad,
Therefore (willing to win worship) is my name:
In the countrey there is none such to be had,
And the Court doth aske, great cost for the same.
So that what I shall doe, I know not yet,
I consider it is toward a good time:
Wherein tryumphing is vsed, as is moste fit,
And where Courtyers must shew themselues, braue and (fine.
But this I conclude, as forced I am,
The Court for to leaue, and homeward to packe:
For where is the money? here is the man,
If man he may be, that money doth lacke.

Corage. ¶ Syr are you so foolish, the Court for to leaue?
When the time is, that worship you should win:
For in times of tryumphing, we alwayes perceaue,
The Courtyers worship, doth first begin.
Therefore do you from such foolishnesse stay,
And Fortune may chaunce, giue you as you wish.

Courtyer. ¶ But the wheeles of Fortune, as Socrates doth say,
Are like the snares, wherewith men take fish.
And in an other place, Plautus doth shew,
A saying in Laten, and that is this:
Festo die si quid prodigeris,
Profesto egere liceat nisi pepereris,
If on the Holiday, wasting thou doe vse,
On the worke day thou mayest beg, vnlesse well thou get:
So in tryumphing, like effect insues,
That next after waste, indigence is set.

Corage. ¶ Then Perianders wordes you accoumpt least,
Who vnto honour, an incorager is:
Honor (sayeth he) Immortalis est,
Now syr I pray you, how like you this?

Courtyer. ¶ Those wordes to be true, I must needes confesse,
For honour in deede, is an immortall fame:

And now is the time the same to possesse,
But I haue not wherewith to atchiue the same.
For money is he that the man must decke,
And though I haue attire both costly and gay,
Yet vnlesse it be new, I shall haue but a geck,
Therefore much better for me be away.

Corage. ¶Tush man for money be thou not sad,
You Courtyers I know haue Jewels good store,
And money for Jewels will alwayes be had,
Therefore for that matter care thou no more.

Courtyer. ¶Yea but how it is had, I partely doe know,
And what excessiue interrest is payde,
Therefore you may say the more is my woe,
Would God that I had it neuer assayde.

Corage. ¶Well, what euer it cost, it must neédes be had,
Therefore withstand not thy fortunate chaunce,
For I will count theé foole, worse then mad,
If thou wilt not spend money, thy selfe to aduaunce,
Now is the time of hap good or ill:
Venture it therefore while it is hote,
For the Tyde will not tarry for any mans will,
Neuer shalte thou speéde, if now thou speéde not.

Courtyer. ¶Truely this talke doth encorage me so much,
That to seé the Court agayne, I doe pretend,
But I pray theé doest thou know any such,
As vse vpon gages money to lend?

Corage. ¶Why man for that matter you neéde not to doubt,
Of such men there are ynow euery where,
But seé how luckely it doth fall out.
Seé yonder two friendes of mine doe appeare.
There is a broker betweéne man and man,
When as any bargaynes they haue in hand,
The other a Marchauntes man now and than,
In borrowing money, thy friendes they may stand.

Helpe and Furtheraunce enter.

¶So

Helpe. ¶So are we in déede, and what of that?
Who is it that with vs would any thing haue?
Courtyer. ¶Euen I a Gentleman whome money doe lack,
And therein your friendſhip would gladly craue.
Helpe. ¶Therein we can helpe you if your pleaſure it be,
And will do or elſe we were greatly to blame,
Prouided alwayes that to our paynes you doe ſée,
And alſo put in a good pawne for the ſame.
Courtyer. ¶A pawne ſufficient I will therefore lay,
And alſo your paynes I will recompence well,
But I muſt néedes haue it out of the way,
Although my Landes therefore I do ſell.
Helpe. ¶You ſhall haue it ſyr ſo ſoone as you will,
And therein you ſhalbe friendly vſed,
For in friendly vſing this fellow hath ſkill, pointing to Fur-
Therefore his counſel muſt not be refuſed. theraunce,
He is ſeruaunt vnto a Marchaunt man,
Who is partly ruled after his minde.
Courtyer. ¶In déede as you ſay, helpe me he can,
I doubt not but his friendſhip I ſhall fynd.
Doubt you not ſyr, but in pleaſuring me,
I will recompence your paynes with the moſte.
Further. ¶What I can doe for you, ſoone you ſhall ſée,
It is but folly thereof for to boaſt.
Courtyer. ¶Well then it is time that hence we were packing,
For fayne an end thereof I would know.
Helpe. ¶Why ſyr no dilligence in vs ſhalbe lacking,
For we are ready, if that you be ſo.
Courtyer. ¶Why then that we go I thinke it were beſt,
Thinke you your mayſter is now at home?
Further. ¶Ye I know well at home he doth reſt,
And I geſſe that now he is ſitting alone,
Therefore no longer here let vs ſtay.
Courtyer. ¶Then ſir adew for I will leade the way.
Speaking to Corage & goeth out with Furtherance, & Helpe.

C.iij. ¶Now

Corage. ¶ Now may you see how Corage can worke,
And how he can encorage, both to good and bad:
The Marchaunt is incouraged, in greedinesse to lurke,
And the Courtyer to win worship, by Corage is glad.
The one is good, no man will denay,
I meane corage to win worship and fame:
So that the other is ill, all men will say,
That is corage to greedinesse, which getteth ill name.
Thus may you see Corage contagious,
And eake contrarious, both in me do rest:
For I of kind, am allwayes various,
And chaunge, as to my mind seemeth best.
Betweene man and wife, sometimes I doe showe,
Both my kindnesse, when my pleasure it is:
The goodwife giueth her husband a blow,
And he for reward, doth giue her a kisse.
The goodwyfe by Corage, is hardy and stoute,
The goodman contrary, is pacient and meeke:
And suffreth himselfe to be called loute,
Yea, and worse misused, thrise in a weeke.
How say you good wiues, is it not so?
I warrant you, not one that can say nay:
Whereby all men here, may right well know,
That all this is true which I doe say.
But yet Corage tels you not all that he knowes,
For then he must tell, of ech wife the name:
Which is no greate matter, the best are but shrewes,
But I will not say so, for feare I haue blame.

Greedinesse enter.

Greedines ¶ Now Corage I say, what newes in the coste?
What good tidinges abroade, doest thou heare?
Corage. ¶ Why what doest thou heare? hye thee home in poste,
For I sent home a Gentleman, to seeke for thee there.
Greedines ¶ And what is the matter that with me he would haue?

He

Corage. ¶He must borrow some money, his worship to saue.
Greedines ¶Tush then to tarry he will be glad,
If that he come any money to borrow.
Corage. ¶Yea but take the time, while it is to be had,
And deferre not thy profite, vntill to morrow.
This Gentleman is a Courtyer braue,
And now in neede of money doth stand:
Therefore thine owne asking, of him thou mayest haue,
So that thou wilte pleasure him out of hand.
Greedines ¶And is he a Courtyer, and standeth in neede,
This to my purpose, doth rightly fall:
For the needy Courtyers, my cofers do feede,
And I warrant thee, that pinch him I shall.
For since I know, his neede to be such,
That money he must needes occupy:
I know I cannot aske him to much,
If I his mind will satisfy.
Therfore now Corage to thee adew. Fayne a going out.
Corage. ¶Nay softe syr yet one word with you.
You told me not yet how you did agree,
With no good Neighbourhood, that good man growte.
Greedines ¶Mary syr he hath gone thorow with mee,
And the old Tenaunt he will thrust oute.
But I with that matter haue naught to doe,
Let them two now for that agree:
I know I should neuer haue come vnto,
So much as therefore he hath payed to mee.
Therefore I might be counted mad,
If I to his proffer would not haue tended:
This profitable lesson which of thee I had,
The Tyde taryeth no Man, was not vnremembred.
Profite entreth.
Profite. ¶God speede syr, I pray you shew me if you can,
Did you not mayster Welthinesse here about see.
Corage. ¶Cockes passion this is the Gentlemans man,
Speaking to Greedines.

C.iiij. Which

Which at home doth tarry for thée,
Syr Welthinesse is not hence far away.

Turning to Profite.

Greedines ¶I am hée syr, what would you of me require?
Profite. ¶My mayster at home for your worship doth stay,
And to speake with you he doth greatly desyre.
If it be your pleasure home to repayre,
Or if ye will, he shall hether come,
Your maysterships pleasure therefore declare,
And I know incontinent it shalbe done.
Greedines ¶Nay I meane homeward to hye,
For that I suppose to be the best,
And by all the meanes that in me doth lye,
I will fulfill your maysters request.
Profite. ¶I trust also you will consider my payne,
Thereby I trust you shall not lœse,
For perchaunce I may preferre your gayne,
By meane which with my mayster I doe vse.
Greedines ¶As I fynd thée ready in furthering of me,
So doubt thou not but thou shalt fynd,
Me euen as ready in pleasuring of thée,
A word is ynough, thou knowest my minde,
Therefore hence let vs now take the way.
Profite. ¶My mayster thinketh vs long I dare say. Exiunt.
Corage. ¶I warrant you I will not be long behind,
I know no cause why here I should stay,
A company of my schollers I know where to fynd,
Therefore toward them I will take the way. Exiunt.

The Tenaunt tormented entreth.

Tenaunt. ¶Whether shall I goe, or which way shall I take,
To fynd a Christian constant and iust,
Ech man himselfe a Christian would make.
Yet few or none, that a man may trust.

But

But for the most parte fayned, inclined to lust.
As to insaciable couetousenesse, moste abhominable,
Or some other vice, moste vile and detestable.
It is well knowen, what rigour doth raigne,
In that cruell tyger, my Landlord Gréedinesse:
Who in my house, would not let me remayne,
But hath thrust me out, with spitefull spéedinesse,
Hauing no respect, to my naked néedinesse,
But altogether, regarding his gayne,
Hath bereaued my liuing from me, to my payne.
What neighbourhood is, may also be séene,
My neighbour supposed, is my deadly foe:
What cruell chaunce, like to mine hath béene,
Both my house and liuing, I must now forgoe.
What neighbour is he, that hath serued me so:
Thus crewelly to take my house, ouer my head,
Wherein these forty yeares, I haue bene harbored and fed,
And now being aged, must thus be thrust out,
With mine unpotent wife, charge, and famely:
Now how I shall liue, I stand in great dout,
Leading and ending, my life in misery,
But better doe so, then as they liue, by théeuery,
Catching and snatching, all that euer they can,
Because that (say they) Tyde taryeth no Man.
But God graunt that they, in following that Tyde,
Lose not the tyde of Gods mercy and grace:
I doubt that from them, away it will slyde,
If they still pursue the contrary race.
As dayly they doe, Gods lawes to deface,
To their own soules hurte, and to their neighbours damage,
Still following the instructions, of cursed Corage.
I sée whome I séeke, is not here to be found,
I meane Christianity, constant and iust:
I doubte that in bondage he lyeth fast bound,
Or else he is dead, and lyeth buryed in dust.
But if he be liuing, to fynd him I trust,

D.j. Therefore

Therefore till I fynd him, I will no where stay,
Neyther in seeking of him, I will make delay.

Enter Corage.

Corage. ¶Ah syrra, I cannot chose but reioyce,
When I remember my little pretty boyes,
My schollers I meane, who all with one voyce,
Crye we loue Corage, without other choyce.
The yong ympes I incorage and leade,
In ryotous footesteps, so trimly to treade.
That guilty, and vnguilty, often they pleade,
And being found guilty, hang all saue the head.
The virgins which are but tender of age,
Rather then their trim attyre should swage.
Their tayles for new they will lay to gage,
To euery slaue, peasaunt, and page.
The grand signyoures, which in yeares are rype,
With couetous clawes, like the greedy grype.
Their poore brethren, from their liuinges do wype,
And euermore daunce, after Corages pype.
Corage neuer in quiet doth lye,
But the Tyde taryeth no man, still he doth crye,
Therefore worke thy will by and by,
That rich thou mayest be, when euer thou dy.

The mayd willfull Wanton enter.

Wanton. ¶Of all misfortunes, mine is the worst,
Truely I thinke I was accurst:
When I was an infant, not fully nurst,
Alas for griefe, my harte it will burst.
I dayly see women as yong as I,
Which in whyte Caps, our dore doe go by:
I am as able as they, with a man to lye,
Yet my mother doth still, my wedding denye.

She

She sayeth for wedding, that I am vnfit,
Maydes of fowerteene yeares she sayeth, hath no wit:
And so euery day she sayeth I shall tarry yet,
That would God I were put quick in the pit.
God wot we maydes, abide much misery,
And alwayes kept in, from hauing liberty:
Of euill tongues we walke in ieoberty,
Most people are now so full of ielousy:
If a yongman a mayde doe but kisse,
Now (say the people) you may see what she is:
Where if I were a wyfe, nothing I should misse,
But liue like a Lady, in all ioyfull blisse.
I right well doe know, the peoples spight,
Because that to be pleasaunt, I haue delight:
Therefore past grace, they say I am quight,
And a wilfull wanton, my name they doe wright.
Yet I trust in God, once to see the day,
That to recompence their spight I may:
For if euer I be marryed, and beare any sway,
Then I know what I haue to say.
Therefore good God, make me shortly a wife,
Or else shortly take away my life.

Corage. ¶ Alas prety Parnell, you may soone end this stryfe,
Yong men fit for husbandes, in this towne are ryfe.
And your mothers ill will, you may soone preuent,
If you will follow my councell, and intent.

Wanton. ¶ Oh but if my mother would thereto consent,
To be marryed this night, I could be content.

Corage. ¶ But consent she or not, yet is it for thee,
Unto thine own preferment to see.
Doest thou with any yong man so agree,
That he would consent, thy husband to bee.

Wanton. ¶ Dyuers there are, who gladly would haue me,
And being their wyfe, would trimly bebraue me.
From all wrong they would defend and saue me,
Tush ynowe there are, which to wife doe craue me.

 ¶ Thes

Corage. ¶ Then deferre no time if that thou be wise,
For now to preferment, thou arte like to arise.
The Tide taryeth no man, else the prouerbe lyes,
In delaying comes harmes, thou seeest with thine eyes.
But by mariage all thy greefe shalbe eased,
And thy ioyes shall manifold wayes be increased.

Wanton. ¶ But alas my mother will so be displeased,
That I know her wrath will neuer be appeased.

Corage. ¶ And wilt thou for displeasing of her,
Thine owne preferment and fortune defer?
Now arte thou youthfull, thy selfe to prefere,
And thy youthfull bewty, mens heartes may stere.
But youthfull bewty will not alwayes last,
The Tyde taryeth no man, but soone it is past,
Therefore to wedding, see thou make haste,
For now much time thou doest lose in waste.

Wanton. ¶ Oh what comfortable wordes are these,
Truely your talke doth me greatly please,
I will not stinte but seeke out alwayes,
Untill that I haue found some ease.
I care not what my mother doe say,
This matter I will no longer delay.
But a husband I will haue out of the way,
And then may I boldly dally and play.
No man dare me then once to controule,
Least my husband chaunce for to scoule.
If any man vse to intreate me foule,
My husband will lay him ouer the noule.
It doth me good to thinke of the blisse,
Which betweene new marryed couples is.
To see their dallyaunce sometime ywisse,
It setteth my teeth an edge by gisse.
Truely I would gladly giue my best frock,
And all thinges else vnto my smock.
To be marryed in the morning by vj. of the clock,
I beshrew my heart if that I doe mock.

Syr you will not beleeue how I long,
To be one of the wedded throng.
My thinkes it lyeth in no tongue,
To shew the ioyes that is them among.

Corage. ¶ It passeth ioy which they imbrace,
They take their pleasure in euery place.
Like Aungels they doe run their race,
In passing blisse, and great solace.

Wanton. ¶ Well syr I will no longer tarry,
But some man out of hand will marry.
Although from my mothers minde I varry,
Yet your wordes in minde I carry.
Therefore good sir to you adew,
Untill agayne I meete with you.
If I speede well, a good coate new,
To your parte may chaunce insue. *Exiunt.*

Corage. ¶ Alas wilfull wanton, my pretty peate,
My wordes haue set her in such a heate.
Now toward wedding her loue is so greate,
That scarce she can neither drinke nor eate.
Now I Corage in her doe begin,
So that for her mother she cares not a pin,
Now all her mind is a husband to win,
To be unwedded she thinketh it sin.
How say you my virgines euery one,
Is it not a sinne to lye alone?
When .xij. yeares of age is gone,
I dare say you thinke so euery one.

Helpe entereth.

Helpe. ¶ Nay now let him shifte for himselfe if he will,
Since I am payed the thing I did seeke:
Alas good Gentleman, he is serued but ill,
In fayth he is in now by the weeke.
He hath naught but that, for which he hath payed,

D.iij. The

The loue of his money he hath dearly bought,
I warrant you it might be boldly ſayd,
His cardes being tolde, he hath wonne right nought.
Corage. ¶And how ſo Helpe? is he ſo pincht I ſay?
By my troth that is a ſport for to heare.
Helpe. ¶Serra, he ſtandes bound forty poundes to pay,
But little more then thirty away he did beare,
For what with the marchauntes duety for lone,
Item for writing vnto the ſcrybe:
The third part into my pouch is gone,
And the marchauntes man, hath not loſt his brybe.
So that amongeſt vs folwer, almoſt ten poundes,
Is clearely diſperſed and ſpent:
The Gentleman ſweareth, harte, blood, and woundes,
Repenting that after thy councell he went.
Corage. ¶Yea but ſyrs, my parte is the leaſt,
Who am the Captayne of all the route.
Helpe. ¶Tuſh man for that matter, ſet thy heart at reſt,
For that which we haue, thou ſhalt not be without,
But ſyrra, ſeeſt thou not who doth yonder appeare,
By my troth me thinkes two knaues they are.

Profite and Furtheraunce, enter together.

Further. ¶Indeede whoſoeuer vnto thee is neare,
For a knaue he needeth not to ſeeke farre.
Corage. ¶Sirs I will tell troth to make you agree,
By geſſe I thinke, you are knaues all three.
Further. ¶In deede three we are, we are no leſſe,
And you are the fourth to make vp the meſſe.
Corage. ¶Well for that matter, we will not greatly ſtriue,
But ſyrs what wind now did you hether driue?
Further. ¶I fayth to ſhew thee what luck we haue had,
By (Willing to win Worſhip) that luſty lad.
To make talke thereof, now it is no time,
But if thou wilt go with vs, we will giue thee the wine.

¶And

Profite. ¶And as my mayster pleased you two, and the scribe,
So of Grædinesse the Marchaunt, I had a bribe,
So that none of vs went vacant away,
But of one of the parties, had honestly our pay.
Helpe. ¶Yea but of them both, I had my bribes,
My maysters, the Broker can play of both sides.
He is almost payd as well for his trotting,
As is the Scribe, for his writing or blotting.
Yea and yet both parties are not content,
For I dare say the gentleman, his bargayne doth repent.
Further. ¶Marry syr can you blame him, that so hath bene rung,
He may say he hath payde, to heare a faire tongue.
And now without his man he is gone,
His man geues him leaue for to walke alone.
Profite. ¶Let me alone, I warrant thée some excuse I will haue,
And the worst fall I know, I shalbe but called knaue.
But yet sirs after him, I will hye,
And by the way I will inuent some lye.
Corage. ¶Nay softe Profyte, you must not go so,
You must helpe to sing a parte or you goe.
Profite. ¶So it be short, I am well content.
Corage. ¶And all the residue thereto do consent.

The Song.

WE haue great gayne, with little payne,
And lightly spend it to:
We doe not toyle, nor yet we moyle,
As other pore folkes do.
We are winners all thrée,
And so will we bée,
Where euer that we come a,
For we know how,
To bend and bow,
And what is to be done a,
With, ¶To

¶ To knéele and crouch, to fill the pouch,
We are full glad and fayne:
We euer still, euen at our will,
Are getters of great gayne.
We are winners. &c.

¶ It is our will, to poule and pill,
All such as doe vs trust:
We beare in hande, good friendes to stand,
Though we be most vniust.
We be winners. &c.

¶ Full far aboutes, we know the routes,
Of them that riches had:
Whome through deceite, as fysh to bayte,
We made their thrift forth gad.
We are winners. &c.

Finis.

Corage. ¶ Now Cole profite, in fayth gramarcy for thy song.
Profite. ¶ Much good do it thée, but I am afeard I tarry to long.
Therefore friendes adue, for I will be gone.
Helpe. ¶ Nay softe Profite, leaue vs not behind,
For hence to depart, we also do minde.
Corage. ¶ Then thrée knaues on a cluster, get you together,
Néedes knaues you must go, for so you came hether.
Profite. ¶ But here we found thée, a knaue most of all,
And so we leaue thée, as thou doest vs call.
Corage. ¶ Now so is the purpose, and this is the case,
Good cosen Cutpurse, if you be in place.
I beséech you now, your businesse to plye,
I warrant thée I, no man shall thée espye.
If they doe, it is but an howers hanging,
But such a purse thou mayest catch, worth a yeres spending.
I warrant thée encouraging thou shalt not lack,
Come hyther, let me clap thée on the back.

And

And if thou wilt now follow my request,
At Tyborne I may chaunce clap thee on the brest.
So that of clapping, thou shalt haue store,
Here clapping behind, and at Tyborne before.
But cosen Cutpurse, if ought thou do get,
I pray thee let me haue part of thy cheate.
I meane not of thy hanging fare,
But of thy purse, and filched share.
Well syrs it is time, that hence I doe pack me,
For I am afrayde, that some men doe lack me.
For some are perhaps, about some good deede,
And for lack of corage, they dare not proceede. Exiunt.

The Courtyer entreth.

Courtyer. ¶As with the poyson, which is moste delectable,
The heart of man, is soonest infected:
So the foe moste hurteth, who seemeth most amiable,
And of all wise men, is to be detected.
At this time this saying I haue elected,
For that they which friendship, to me professed,
In steade thereof, my hurte haue addressed.
They promised me, my friendes for to stand,
And to helpe me to that which I did craue:
Untill that I had obligated my land,
And then was I subiect to euery knaue,
Ech man then a porcion would haue,
The Marchaunt for lone, the Broker for his payne,
And the scrybe for wryting, ech man had a gayne.
Ninubula pluuia imbrem parit,
A mizeling shower ingendreth great wet,
Which saying officium prouerbia non tarit,
Many a little maketh a great.
So euery of them, by me wrought his feate,
And euery of these brybes, being cast to account,
To a good porcion I feele do amount.

E.j. But

But what vilany is there in such,
Who knowing a man, of their helpe to haue neede:
Will incroch vpon him, so vnreasonable much,
Their owne greedy desires to feede.
Iuuenall I remember, doth teach them in deede,
Whose wordes are these, both open and playne,
The vicious man only, seeketh his own gayne:
Yea twice vicious, may they be named,
Who doe auarice so much imbrace:
But what is their aunswere, when they are blamed,
Say they, we haue here but a little space.
Therefore we haue neede to be getting a pace,
Wherefore should we gayning lay away,
The Tyde taryeth no Man, this is all they can say.

Corage entereth.

Corage. ¶And as sone as she had supped vp the broth,
The ladle she layd vpon his face:
Woman quoth he, why arte thou so wroth?
Knaue quoth she, get thee out of this place.

And smyteth the gentleman.

Courtyer. ¶Why friend, arte thou not well in thy wit,
Wherefore smitest thou me in such sorte?

Corage. ¶Iesus Gentleman, are you here yet,
I thought long or this you had bene at the Courte,
Therefore you must pardon mine offence,
For I little thought it had bene you.

Courtyer. ¶Thy company is so good, I will get me hence,
Therefore cursed Corage adue.

Corage. ¶And in fayth will you neede be gon,
What man you might tarry a while.

Courtyer. ¶In thy company I haue tarryed to long,
For I perceaue thou art full of guile. Exiunt.

Corage. ¶Farewell frost, will you neede be gone,
Adue since that you will needes away:
In fayth this sporte is trimsy alone,

That

That I can thus, a gentleman fray.

Greedinesse and Helpe enter together.

Greedines ¶Oh Helpe, might I once see that day,
Tush I would not care, who I did wrong.
Helpe. ¶Doubt not, you neede not that for to fray,
You shall see that day, or that it be long.
Corage. ¶What day is that, whereof you doe speake?
May not a body your councell know.
Helpe, ¶Mary syr, this day whereof we doe intreate,
Is a day of some notable show.
When the Courtyers in their brauery shalbe,
Before their Prince, some shew to make:
If such a day, Welthinesse might see,
He hopeth then, some money to take.
For without cost, they may not be braue,
And many lacke money, as he doth suppose:
Wherefore at some, a good hand he would haue,
I warrant thee, by none he hopeth to lose.
Corage. ¶Tush man doubt not, such dayes there will come,
That matter thou needest not to feare.
Greedines ¶To here of such dayes, I would ryde and run,
So glad I would be, of such dayes to heare.
Oh with these Courtyers, I loue to deale well,
Or with other yong Gentlemen, who haue pounds or lands:
For whether I doe lend them, or my wares to them sell,
I am sure to win largely, at their handes.
And specially, where in neede they doe stand,
Then in fayth I doe pinch them home:
When I see they must needes haue money out of hand,
And that other shifte, to worke they haue none.
Helpe. ¶Why that is the way syr to come alofte,
Great welth thereby, I know you doe get.
Greedines ¶I warrant thee no time, I driue of,
Neyther for any mans saying, the same will I let.

Well syrs I must now leaue of this talke,
And I must bid you both twayne adue. *Fayne a going out.*
Corage. ¶Softe mayster Greedinesse whether do you walke,
What syr I pray you, one word with you.
Greedines ¶Towardes Powles Crosse, from hence I doe goe,
Perchaunce some profite there I may meete.
Corage. ¶To Powles Crosse, what there will you doe,
Do you the Preachers wordes so well like.
Greedines ¶Tush for the preaching I passe not a pin,
It is not the matter wherefore I do go:
For that goeth out whereas it comes in,
But herein my meaning, to thee I will show,
You know that many thether doe come,
Wherefore perchaunce, such may be my hap:
Of my ill debtors there to spye some,
Whome without delay, by the heeles I will clap.
Helpe. ¶Why syr, and will you arest them there:
While they at sermon preaching be.
Greedines ¶Will I quoth you, wherefore should I feare,
It is best taking them, while I may them see.
Corage. ¶Yea bir Lady syr, full wisely you say,
Take them while you may them get:
Or else perchaunce it wilbe many a day,
Or on them agayne your eye you shall set.
Greedines ¶I remember what you haue sayd,
Tyde taryeth no man, marke you that:
Wherefore no time herein shalbe delayed,
Therefore syrs adew to long I do chat. *Exiunt.*
Corage. ¶Now that here is none but you and I,
I pray thee deliuer to me my part,
Dispatch and geue me it by and by:
And that I say with a willing hart,
Helpe. ¶I know no part I haue of thine,
Therefore of me thou gettest no part.
Corage. ¶I will make thee confesse a parte of mine,
Or else I will make thy bones to smart.

¶When

Helpe. ¶When the reſidue doe thereto agrée,
Then will I alſo geue thée a parte:
But if they no part will giue vnto thée,
If I giue thée any, beſhrew my harte.
Corage. ¶Yea friend Helpe, are you at that poynt,
I will make you otherwiſe to ſay:
Or elſe I will heate you in euery ioynt,
Now mayſter Helpe, how like you this play.

And fighteth to prolong the time, while Wantonneſſe maketh her ready.

Helpe. ¶What hold thy hand man, arte thou ſo mad,
Corage. ¶To confeſſe me a part, I will make thée glad.
Helpe. ¶A parte thou ſhalt haue, when home we doe come.
Corage. ¶Vpon that condicion mine anger is done.
A ſyrra th inke you, to make me your knaue,
And yet all the profite your ſelues you would haue.

Enter waſtfulneſſe the huſband of Wantonneſſe.

Waſtful. ¶What ioy is like the linked life?
What hope might hold me from my wife?
Can man his tongue ſo frame,
Or eke diſpoſe me from my dame?
What doth my ſubſtaunce good to mée,
I will therefore be franke and frée.
Where couples yong do méete,
That plyaunt péece ſo ſwéete.
My ioy for to declare,
Whoſe bewty is ſo rare.
In cofers lockt to lye,
To ſerue my wyfe and I.
Corage. ¶Then doe you wiſely, I ſweare by S. Anne
Take time while time is, for time will away;
The niggard is neuer counted a man.

Therefore remember to doe as you say.
Wastful. ¶ I warrant thee, what I haue sayd,
Nothing I meane shalbe delayed.
I will the same fulfill,
To ease and please my will.
Helpe. ¶ Truely syr you doe wisely therein,
For what good of hoording insues:
Undoubtedly I thinke it a sinne,
And beastes they are, which the same doe vse.
Wastful. ¶ Use it who list, for me he shall, I meane to hoord no store,
I meane to serue my time withall, and then I seeke no more.

Wantonnesse enter.

Wanton. ¶ Jesus husband what doe you meane,
To run abroade, and leaue me at home:
You are such a man, as I haue not seene,
I see well, hereafter you will leaue me alone.
That so soone begin, from me to be straying,
What man, it is yet but honny moone.
Wastfull. ¶ What woman would you haue me alwayes playing?
So may we shortly both be vndone.
As for pleasure there is a time,
So for profite there is the like:
Therefore I pray thee gentle wife mine,
Be contented that my profite I seeke.
Wanton. ¶ Yea but husband I say consider in your mind,
That now we are yong, and plyaunt to play:
But age approaching, makes vs lame and blind,
And lusty corage doth then draw away.
Then what may substaunce vs auayle,
For age no pleasure doth regard:
Therefore good sweete harte doe not quayle,
Thinke neuer that the world is hard.
Corage. ¶ Undoubtedly moste true it is.
The woman herein doth truely say:

Sir

Sir haue not you heard before this,
Tyde taryeth no man, but will away.
Wastfull. ¶ But better it is hardly to begin,
And after in better estate to bee:
Then fyrst to be alofte full trim,
And after to fall to lower degrée.
Wanton. ¶ Truely that is but a folish toy,
At the fyrst to liue hardly and bare:
Many we sée misse that hoped ioy,
And then it proueth, for others they spare.
Haue not many had, full sorrowfull hartes,
By losing of that which they did spare:
Had they not better haue taken their partes,
Then so for others, them selues to make bare.
And what know we, if we shall liue,
To take our partes of that we scrape:
Would it not then your harte gréeue,
To leaue your substaunce in such rate.
Wastful. ¶ Yea but swéete harte, if naught we shall haue,
When hereafter we shall aged wax:
Then had we better wish vs in graue,
Then néedy pouerty should vs vex.
Wanton. ¶ Doubt you that such chaunce shall befall,
Truely you are greatly vnwyse:
We are able to kéepe vs from such thrall,
Wastfull. Spend, and God will send, else the prouerbe lyes.
¶ His sending woman, we dayly do sée,
Is a staffe and a wallet vnto such:
Who such excessiue spenders bée,
Experience thereof we haue to much.
Wanton. ¶ Well husband this talke is in vayne,
Therefore cease so sharply to speake:
For vnlesse such talke you doe refrayne,
I feare for vnkindnesse my harte will breake.
I little thought that you would thus,
Haue now restrayned me of my will:

C.iiij. But

But now right well I may discusse, *Shee weepeth.*
That you doe loue some other gill.
Wastful. ¶ Why woman doest thou thinke that I,
Haue thought all this while, as I haue sayd:
I did it onely thy mind to trye,
For pleasure in me, shall not be delayd.
While the time is, the time I will take,
What soeuer I list to say:
Of my goods no God I will make,
Therefore good wife, do thy sorow away.
Wanton. ¶ A fayth are you such a one indeede,
By gisse you made me almost afeard:
My harte in my belly was ready to bleede,
When such foolish wordes in you I heard.
Helpe. ¶ I would haue counted him greatly vnwise,
If he were so foolish, as himselfe he made:
Fooles they are, which such pleasure despise,
But I knew that therein he would not wade.
And truely I am right glad to see,
That so good an agreement betweene you is:
For truely where couples doe so well agree,
It may not be chosen, but there is great blisse.
I am sorry that thus we must parte you froe,
Corage it is time for vs to departe.
Wanton. ¶ But yet my friendes before that you goe,
Of a song helpe vs to sing a parte.
By my troth husband we must needes haue a song,
Will you not helpe to further the same?
Wastful. ¶ Yes by my troth, so it be not long,
Or else you might count me greatly to blame.
Corage. ¶ And I am content a part for to beare.
Helpe. ¶ Then be sure I will helpe in with a share.

The Song.

¶ Though

Though Wastfulnesse and wantonnesse,
Some men haue vs two named:
Yet pleasauntnesse and plyauntnesse,
Our names we haue now framed.
For as I one is pleasaunt, to kisse and to cully,
The other is plyaunt as euer was holly.
As youth would it haue,
So will we be braue.

¶ To liue in blisse, we will not misse,
What care we for mens sayings:
What ioy is this, to sporte and kisse,
But hurte comes in delayings.
The one is full ready to the others becking,
Betwéene vs there is neither chiding, nor checking.
As youth will it haue, &c.

¶ Full braue and full fyne, we passe the time,
Take time while time is byding:
What ioy is thine, the same is mine,
My mind shall not be slyding.
Our goods are our owne, why should we spare,
Or for time to come, why should we care.
As youth would it haue, &c.

Corage. ¶ Now friendes adue for we must depart,
Wastfull. ¶ Farewell my gentle friendes withall my hart.
Wanton. ¶ Well husband now I will home repayre,
To sée that your dinner dressed be. Exiunt.
Wastful. ¶ Doe so wife, and sée we haue good fare,
I meane not long to tarry after thée. Pause.
Whose ioy may be compared to mine,
I haue a wife bewtifull and gay:
She is yong, pleasaunt, proper and fyne,
And plyaunt to please me both night and day.
For whome should I pinch, for whome should I spare,

F.j. Why

Why should I not be liberall and free,
How euer the world goe I doe not care.
I haue ynough for my wife and me,
And if my substaunce chaunce to decay:
I know my credite is not so ill,
But that I can borrow twenty pound alway.
To serue me at my pleasure and will,
For repayment thereof, no care I will take:
No matter it is if the same I may get,
While it lasteth, therewith I will merry make.
What skils it though that I come in debt.
While yong I am, youthfull I will be,
And passe my time in youthfull sorte:
For as my wife here sayd vnto me.
Age doth delight in no pleasaunt sport,
Wherefore since pleasure I doe loue:
In youth it behooues to take the same,
Nothing there from my heart shall moue.
But I thereto my heart will frame.
I feare me that I tarry to long,
My wife doe looke for me before this:
Therefore homeward I will be gone,
For there is ioy and heauenly blisse. Exiunt.

The Sergeaunt and the debtor rested entereth.

Debtor, ¶ What infidelity in him doth rest,
Who no time forbeareth to take his pray:
Most like the greedy or sauadge beast,
Who in creuelty rageth both night and day.
Might he not the space of one Sermon stay,
What care or minde gaue he to Gods word,
Who at preaching thereof did me so disturbe.
Is the Sabboth day, and Paules Crosse,
A time and place to vex thy debtor?
Or hast thou Greedinesse by me had any losse?
Nay by me thou arte a hundereth pound the better,
I speake of the least and not of the greatter.

Yet

Yet I neuer denyed, my debt for to pay,
But in deede I requyred a longer day.

Sergeant. ¶ Tush syr this talke is all but in vayne,
Meane you thus the time to delay?
Dispatch therefore, and please me for my payne,
And toward the Counter, let vs away.

Debtor. ¶ No haste but good, stay yet a while,
Or else take the payne with me for to walke:
About the quantity of halfe a mile,
With a friend of mine, that I might talke.

Sergeant. ¶ For a Royall I will not so farre goe,
Therefore set your heart at quyet.

Debtor. ¶ I meane to please no Sergeant so,
I am no customer for your dyet.
But since to goe, you doe not intend,
You must take paynes here to tarry with me:
Untill for a friend of mine I doe send,
Which I trust shortly my bayle will be.

Sergeant. ¶ Neyther will I with thee here remayne,
Therefore dispatch and let vs away:
Thinkest thou that I hauing naught for my payne,
Will eyther goe with thee, or heare for thee stay.

Debtor. ¶ And what wilt thou aske, with me here to stay?
At one word let me that vnderstand.

Sergeant. ¶ At one word ten groates thou shalt pay,
Or else to the Counter we must out of hand.

Debtor. ¶ That will I doe with a right good will,
Rather then so much thou shalt get:
I will not so much thy minde fulfill,
If that my harte, my hand may let.

Sergeant. ¶ Why then with speede let vs away,
This deede thou wilt repent I trow.

Debtor. ¶ Well, wherefore now doe we stay,
I am ready hence to goe.

Sergeant. ¶ Come on then.

They two go out.

F.ij. Christianity

A new Commody called

Chriſtianity muſt enter with a ſword, with a title of pollicy, but on the other ſyde of the tytle, muſt be written gods word, alſo a Shield, wheron muſt be written riches, but on the other ſyde of the Shield muſt be Fayth.

Chriſtian. ¶Chriſtianity I doe repreſent,
Muſe not though the ſword of pollicy I beare:
Neyther marueile not what is mine intent,
That this fayleable ſhield of riches I weare.
Greedy great, will haue it ſo euery where,
Greedy great for this cauſe I haue named,
For that the greater parte vſe greedines, which is to be (blamed.
As the greater parte will, thereto muſt I yeeld,
Their cruell force I may not withſtand:
Therefore I beare this deformed ſword and ſhield,
Which I may be aſhamed to hold in my hand,
But the Lord deliuer me from their thraldome and band,
For if the enemy aſſayle me, then am I in thrall:
Becauſe I lack ſuch Armoure, as is taught by S. Paule.
For in ſteade of Gods word, and the ſhield of fayth,
I am deformed with pollicy, and riches vayne:
And ſtill I ſay, as the greater parte ſayeth,
I am ſtill a chriſtian, and ſo ſhall remayne,
My Chriſtianity ſay they, no domage doth ſuſtaine:
But alas they are deceiued, their armoure is not ſure,
For neyther pollicy, nor ryches, may long time indure.
Yet vpon thoſe two, we greatly depend,
We ſay by pollicy, our ſelues we can ſaue,
Riches as a ſhield, we ſay will defend,
And by riches we poſſeſſe what euer we craue,
So that for riches, we ſell all that we haue.
Not onely the body, and all thinges tereſtriall,
But alſo the ſoule, which ought be celeſtiall.

Faythfull few enter.

Faythfull. ¶Alas I lament to heare the report,
Which of vs cittizens in euery place is ſpread:
It is not long ſynce I came from the court,

Where

Where I would haue bene glad to haue hid my head.
With the ſpoyle of the ſymple, there they ſay were fed,
So that for the couetous greedines, which ſome cittizens vſe,
A ſhamefull ill reporte to the whole enſues.
But I muſt neede confeſſe ſome among vs there be,
For whoſe ſakes the whole number beareth great blame:
They abuſe themſelues ſo, towardes euery degree,
As man without reaſon, and paſt worldly ſhame,
Neither regard they their owne, nor their ill name.
So they may haue the chaffy treaſure of the world,
They paſſe not both with God and man to be abhord.
There is no time nor place, that they will forbeare,
When any of their helpe hath moſte neede:
Then ſhall he pay treble for his money or ware,
Or elſe of them he is not like to ſpeede.
They nothing regard his pouerty or neede,
But who is it which yonder doth ſtand? he goeth toward him
Holding the Sword of Pollicy in his hand,
Moſte certayne I am, that face I ſhould know,
Syr is not your name Chriſtianity?

Chriſtian. ¶Yes vndoubtedly, my name is ſo,
As you are faythfull few imbraſer of verity.

Faythfull. ¶And ſhall the Sword of Pollicy, by Chriſtianity be borne,
Truely that is contrary to your nature and kinde:
Now are you deformed like a thing forlorne,
Which maketh me ſuſpect, of me in my minde.

Chriſtian. ¶Oh Faythfull fewe, of me haue no doubt,
I am Chriſtianity, though thus deformed:
And though thus abuſed, by the great route,
Yet by God I truſt, my tytle ſhalbe turned.

Faythfull. ¶By the power of God I wil not delay, he turneth the titles
To turne this tytle moſt vntrue and fayned,
And I will indue thee, and that ſtraight way,
With ſuch weapons, as Saynt Paule hath ordayned.

Chriſtian. ¶Alas in vayne this payne you doe take,
For as you faythfull, in number are few,

So tho power is but small that you can make,
To resist the greedy great ones, who are agaynst you.

Faythfull. ¶ Si Deus nobiscum, quis contra nos,
If God be with vs, who may vs resist,
Weigh not then the number, but weigh his purpose,
Who ruleth all thinges, as himselfe doth list.
I know how Greedinesse, with the great part is vsed,
Their pilling, pouling, pinching and spoyling:
How both the simple and others, with them are abused,
They liue by the fruites of other mens toyling.
But God is not dead, neyther is he a sleepe,
Although for a time his hand he doth hold:
Yet doth he remember his little sheepe,
And will reuenge the wrong done to his folde.

Corage and Greedines enter as though they
saw not Christianity.

Corage. ¶ Let them say what they wil, doe thou as I told thee,
Trust thou not to any knaue of them all:
Not a Preacher of them all, in thy neede will vphold thee,
Try them who will, their deuotion is small.

Greedines ¶ Thou wilt not beleeue how the knaue did prate,
Ye cittizens repent, thus he did crye,
Looke about in time quoth hee, or it be to late,
For the vengeaunce of God at hand is full nye,
As though he knew what were in Gods minde,
Surely it is a shame, they are so suffred to lye.

Corage. ¶ But in my talke great profyte thou doste fynde,
They are all lyers as their talke doth trye,
By my doctrine thou haste great profyte and gayne,
Great riches and substaunce, therby thou doest win:
To instruct thee dayly I take great payne,
Which way thou shalt thy riches bring in.

Greedines ¶ Thou doest so in deede, and thankes I thee giue,
But syrra, now I remember a thing:
Which made me not long since, to laugh in my sleeue,
To me a yong Gentleman the Broker did bring,

Whose

Whose Father was dead of late as it seemed,
And his landes in Morgage to a Marchaunt was layde,
Wherefore it behoued the same were redeemed,
For the day was at hand, when the same should be payde.
And I perceauing his neede to be such,
I thought I would pinch him or that I went,
To giue mine owne asking, he did not greatly grudge,
And when I had girded him, thence I him sent.

Faythfull. ¶More shame for thee, and such as thou art,
That with life thou arte permitted, it is great pitty,
Thou arte a Christyan with a canckered heart,
And the cause of reproch to a whole citty.
Christianity by thee is greatly abused,
Of his righteous Armour, thou doest him bereaue,
And in stead thereof, by him to be vsed,
The Armour of Sathan, with him thou doste leaue.

Greedines ¶Why would you not haue me, how to inuent,
Which way were best to bring in my gayne?

Faythfull. ¶But not in such sort, to set thine intent,
That all the world of thee should complayne.

Greedines ¶I crye you mercy, I know where you are now.
In a Courtyers behalf, this oration you make,
Of late there was one, complayned how,
Excessiue gayne of him I did take.
It is the cast of them all so to say,
When prodigally their money is spent:
Or if the Prince will them not pay,
Then on the Marchaunt, some lyes they inuent.

Faythfull. ¶Arte thou not ashamed of thy Prince to speake ill?
Thine owne abused doing to excuse:
No marueyle though the citty haue all mens ill will,
When both in word and deede, thy selfe thou doest misvse.
Sed Reginum est male,audire cum befecerint,
Antisthenes doth truely this saying resite,
It is geuen to Princes (sayeth he) though they be beneuolēt,
To be euell spoken of which is agaynst all right.

Greedines ¶Syr you are beſt ſay no more, then you are able to proue,
Leaſt I make you to repent your boldneſſe,
For if my pacience you to much do moue,
I may chaunce turne your heate into a coldneſſe.
Why I lende my money like a friend for good will,
And thereby doe helpe men at their neede.

Faythfull. ¶A friend thou arte in deede, though a friend but ill,
Pithagoras thy friendſhip, hath playnely decreede,
There be many ſayth he, who no friendes do lacke,
And yet of friendſhip they haue but ſkant,
So thou arte a friend for their moneys ſake,
And yet thy friendſhip they allwayes ſhall want.

Chriſtian. ¶Aſſuredly thou highly offendeſt,
For that ſo double in dealing thou arte:
Ariſtotle ſayeth, by the ſame thou pretendeſt,
And not ſo to beare a diſſembling harte.
A Chriſtian ought not vnto riches to yeeld,
For it is a thing but fayleable and vayne,
Riches is no perpetuall ſhielde,
But the ſhield of Fayth, ſhall euer remayne.
Take therefore fayth, and Gods word for thy ſworde,
And arme Chriſtianity in this wiſe.

Greedines ¶Shall pollicy and riches then be abhord,
Syr they are fooles that them will deſpiſe.
I put caſe pouerty ſhould me aſſayle,
Can Gods word and fayth me any thing ayde:
Pouerty agaynſt riches can neuer auayle,
I am ſure ſyr this may not be denayde.

Faythfull. ¶We deny not, but in this world, riches beare the ſway,
Yet, it not riches to be called ſure:
For in Gods power it is to make riches decay,
Whereas Gods word and fayth ſhall euer endure.

Greedines ¶But geue me riches, take you Gods word and fayth,
And ſee which of vs ſhall haue the better gayne.

Chriſtian. ¶Now Faythfull few, you here what he ſayth,
Therefore to turne the tytles I muſt be fayne,

Well

Faythfull. ¶ Wel! ſince it will no better be,
To God let vs the cauſe betake:
Whome I truſt, when as time he doth ſee,
He will foꝛ vs, a deliueraunce make.

Corage. ¶ Come Mayſter Welthineſſe, let vs away,
What ſhould we here any longer doe:

Greedines ¶ In deede I hold it beſt as you ſay,
Therefoꝛe your ſaying I agree vnto. They two go out.

Faythfull. ¶ Soꝛry I am, to ſee his eſtate,
Now neare he is, to the Founte of perdition:
God graunt him repentaunce, oꝛ it be to late,
That of his ſinnes he may haue remiſſion.

Chriſtian. ¶ But alas, he goeth the contrary way,
Foꝛ of his couetouſneſſe, he taketh no ruth:
And Ariſtotle I remember doth ſay,
The couetous man cannot learne the truth.
Wherefoꝛe he cannot, oꝛ will not know,
The way to refoꝛme me Chriſtianity:
Therefoꝛe from this place now I will goe,
To pꝛay vnto God to ſhew him the verity.
Now Faythfull fewadue vnto thee,
I will pꝛay vnto God foꝛ thy comfoꝛt and ayd:
I beſeech thee make like interceſſion foꝛ me,
And that my refoꝛmation be not long delayd. Exiunt,

Faythfull. ¶ Doubt not thereof good Chꝛiſtianity,
My indeuour herein ſhall not be delayde:
Alas what is man not knowing the verity,
No man, but a beaſt he may be ſayd.
Yet many there are, which in the woꝛld doth liue,
Who foꝛ Chꝛiſtians will neede accoumpted be:
Though to all abhominations, their ſelues they doe giue,
And from no kind of vice be cleare oꝛ free.
Couetouſneſſe is accoumpted no ſinne,
Vſury is a ſcience and art:
All wayes are good, whereby we may win,
Although it be to our neighbours ſmart.

Whereby it appeareth, from loue we are free,
The wordes of the wise, we nothing regarde:
For without loue, no vertue can perfect bee,
As Plato the wyse, hath playnly declarde.
No good thing without loue, it is possible to doe,
Seneca of that opinyon hath bene:
Then how many good thinges, do they now thinke you,
In whome no loue at all there is seene.
They watch their times, the simple to snare,
No time they forbeare, their pleasures to worke:
God graunt we therefore of them may beware,
For priuily to snare vs, they dayly doe lurke.

Enter Wastfulnesse poorely.

Wastful. Oh more then wretch, which so foolishly hast spent,
Not onely thine own goods, but also other mens:
What accoumpt shall I make, for the goods to me lent,
Which neuer I am able for to recompence.
How wastfully haue I, with wantonnesse my wife,
Consumed our goods, substaunce and treasure,
That would to God I were out of my life,
For the remembraunce thereof, is greefe without measure.
My wyfe and I now, are asunder dispersed,
Ech of vs, to seeke our liuing alone:
Alas our woe may not be rehearsed,
Unto whome now should we make our mone.
In taking the time, to toward we weare,
We were afeard to long to abide:
Corages councell in mind we did beare,
He sayd that for no man would tarry the tyde.
But well away now, which way shall I run,
I know it is folly vnto God to call:
For God I know my peticion will shun,
And into perdition I am now like to fall.
Dispayre, dispayre.

Dispayre enter in some ougly shape, and stand behind him.

Why

Why should I dispayre, since God doth behold,
The sinner with mercy as the Scripture doth say.
Dispa ire. ¶ But thy prodigall sinnes are so manifold,
That God of mercy, doth thee vtterly denay.
Therefore to ende thy life it is best,
Thy calling for mercy, is all but in vayne:
By ending thy life, thou shalt be at rest,
But if longer thou liue, great shall be thy payne.
Wastfull. ¶ Well then will I seeke some place where I may,
Finish my life with Cord, or with knyfe:
The dispatch thereof, I will not delay,
Farewell now all the world, but cheefely my wife. fayne a (going out.
Faythfull few plucketh him agayne.
Faythfull. ¶ Softe stay a whyle, and be not so rash,
Thinkest thou God vnmercifull to be:
Wilt thou trust dispayre, euen at the fyrst dash,
Hast thou no fayth in Gods mercy so free,
Call vpon god with repentaunce and fayth,
By such wayes and meanes as I will instruct thee.
Wastfull. ¶ I beleeue God is mercifull, as the Scripture sayeth.
They both kneele, and Wastfull sayeth after Faythfull.
Faythfull. ¶ Well follow mee, and I will conduct thee.
Oh heauenly Father pardon my offence.
Wastfull. ¶ Oh heauenly father, pardon mine offence.
Faythfull. ¶ And graunt that thy mercy may to me repayre.
Wastfull. ¶ And graunt that thy mercy may to me repayre.
Faythfull. ¶ Also O Father banish thou hence.
Wastfull. ¶ Also O Father banish thou hence.
Faythfull. ¶ That wicked Monster of Dispayre,
Wastfull. ¶ That wicked Monster of Dispayre.
Dispayre flyeth, and they arise.
Faythfull. ¶ How feelest thou now, thy conscience and minde,
Hopest thou not, of gods mercy and grace?
Wastfull. ¶ Well God be praysed that here I thee finde,
How happy was I to approch this place.
Dispayre is now fled, I perfectly know,
G.ij. And

And in Gods mercy I fyrmely doe trust,
Therefore O Lord deliuer me from thrall:
And pardon me a sinner, most vile and vniust.

Faythfull. ¶ That is very well sayd, if so thou doe thinke,
And now frame thy selfe, thy life to amend,
Let dispayre no more into thy mind sincke:
But to be a new man, doe thou now pretend.
And as hertofore thy mind for to please,
Thou haste learned the Tyde will tarry no man,
So now it behoueth for thy greater ease,
That saying, after Gods will for to scan.
Take time while time is, thus I doe meane,
Amend thy life whilst here thou haste space:
To Gods mercifull promises see that thou leane,
So shalt thou enioy the Tide of his grace.

Wastful. ¶ To follow your councell, I will doe my indeuour,
I will seeke the same in all poyntes to performe:
The effect of your wordes I will forget neuer,
And now I will hence, my wife to reforme.
That she and I, in manner new,
May amend our liues, to Gods glory and prayse:
Wherefore good syr vnto you adue,
I beseech the Lord to send thee good dayes. Exiunt.

Faythfull. ¶ See how the time takers their fact doth repent,
Who no time will spare in pleasing their will:
And although the beginning haue a pleasaunt sente,
Yet of the ending, the taste is as ill.
For who euer it be that without measure,
Doth consume his substaunce in prodigall sorte:
Although he had aboundaunce of treasure,
Yet will he be a begger, and that in time shorte.
I marueile where Authority is,
Who should see a helpe for the simple oppressed:
Many thinges there are greatly amisse,
Which by his meanes must needes be redressed.
His absence greatly disquieteth my minde,

I

I will not cease seeking, vntill him I do finde. Exeunt.

Enter Corage weeping.

Corage. ¶Out alas this tydinges are ill,
My friend mayster Greedinesse, hath ended his dayes,
Dispayre vpon him hath wrought his will,
And desperately now he is gone his wayes.
As one enraged and out of his wit,
No remembraunce of God he would haue:
Alas poore man he had a great fit,
Before that well he was layde in his graue. (himselfe.
Why but is Greedines dead in good sadnesse, reasoning with
My thinkes these newes are not true which you tell?
Yes truely he dyed in a great madnesse,
And went with the Tyde boate straight into hell.
Why foole, Greedinesse will neuer dye,
So long as couetous people do liue:
Then you belike doe thinke that I doe lye,
I am as honest a man as any in your sleeue.
I am sure he is dead, or one in his likenesse,
For when he was buryed I stood by:
And some sayd he dyed of the new sicknesse,
Therefore syr thinke not that I doe lye.
For I am as sorry for the death of the man,
As any man that liueth this day:
Wherefore I must needes weepe if I can.
But husht some body is comming this way.

Enter Authority and Faythfull few.

Faythfull. ¶Surely Authority the same is euen he,
I warrant you syr, you neede not to doubt.
Authori. ¶Then wyll we handle him kindly thou shalt see,
Therefore see that from vs hee escape not out.
Corage. ¶God saue your honour, and prosper your estate,
I am glad to see you approch this place:
Those which say ill of you, I vtterly doe hate,
I aunswere for your honour in euery case.
Autho. ¶Ah crafty caytife, why dissemblest thou so?

G.iij. Doest

Doest thou thinke that vs thou mayest so blind,
Thy contagious doinges we right well do know,
And eake thy property, nature and kind.
Thou arte an encorager to all kindes of vice,
The Ages to auaryce, and greedy desyre,
The yonger sorte lack none of thine aduice,
To all such acts as the Deuill doth require.

Corage. ¶ Loe Syr, I thought you did me mistake,
I know right well, the man whome you meane,
To fetch him heather, good speede I will make,
I warrant you, I wil shortly be here agayn. Fayne to go out

Faythfull. ¶ Nay softe he is here, whome that we would haue,
Therefore you neede not him for to fetch.

Corage. ¶ Yes I will fetch him, for he is a very knaue, (out.
And almes it is, that a rope he should stretch. Still fayn to go

Authori. ¶ Upon thy selfe, iust iudgement thou doest giue,
Iuuenall sayeth, Citties are well gouerned,
Whereas such rebelles are now suffered to liue,
But after their desertes, are iustly punished.

Corage. ¶ They which are Rebelles, it behoueth in deede,
That they be corrected and punished so,
For they doe much harme in euery steede,
But I am none such, I would you should know.

Authori. ¶ Thou shalt know what thou art, or hence we depart,
Faythfull sew vpon him lay holde.

Corage. ¶ By gis sir, then I will cause him to smart,
Therefore to touch me, be not so bold.

Faythfull ¶ Syr see where commeth Correction also.

Correction enter.

Autho. ¶ Draw neare Correction and thine office doe,
Take here this caytife vnto the Iayle.

Correcti. ¶ Syr to doe your commaundement I will not fayle,
Come on Syrra and let vs away.

Corage. ¶ Nay softe a whyle your wisedome stay.
Hold me when you haue me, but you haue me not yet,
And perchaunce ere you haue me, your nose I will slit.

¶ Thinkest

Correcti. ¶ Thinkest thou with bragges to make me afeard.
And beginneth to lay handes on him.
Corage. ¶ You are best stand further, least I shaue your beard.
They striue, he draweth his dagger and fyghteth.
Correcti. ¶ In fayth sir, now I wil geue you the check, & catcheth him.
Corage. ¶ Oh gods passyon, wilt thou breake my neck?
Is there no man here that hath a curst wife,
If he will in my stead, he shall end his life.
Correcti. ¶ Tush let vs hence, thy talke is in vayne,
Corage. ¶ Sithens there is no remedy, best is a short payne. Exit.
Faythfull ¶ When all malifactors are duely thus punished,
According to the good and godly lawes,
Then shall Christianity duely be burnished,
And to prayse God, we shall haue cause.
Autho. ¶ O Faythfull few, doubt not but as we,
Are able Christianities estate to reforme:
So his reformation in short time thou shalt see,
For we for his estate doe lament and mourne.
Of our selues we are not able to compasse this thing,
But by this sword of Gods power, which to vs is left:
Wherefore Faythfull few, haue thou no doubting,
But we thereunto doe gladly consent.
For to Socrates saying, some respect we haue,
Who sayeth a citty is not to be praysed,
For the greatnesse of buildings, gorgious and braue,
But for the good inhabitauntes, which therein are placed,
So we accoumpt those countreyes but ill,
Which vicious persons doth mainteine and norish,
Although they haue all thinges at their will,
And although in treasure they aboundauntly florish.
Faythfull ¶ Oh noble Authority, by this your occasion,
Great tranquillity to vs shall befall:
We shalbe a ioy to ech godly nation,
When Christianity is deliuered from thrall.
For better it were vnchristened to be,

Then our Christianity for to abuse:
The Iewish Infidel to God doth more agree,
Then such as Christianity do so misuse.
But see yonder where he doth appeare,
Whose abused armour doth greatly oppresse.

Christianity enter in as at the fyrst.

Authour. ¶ O Christianity vnto vs draw neare,
That we thy abused estate may redresse.
And as freely as this power vnto vs is lent,
Here we now by force of the same:
To these faythfull few do here condescent,
That thou Christianities estate shalt frame.
In such good forme, fashion, and shape,
As the same shall not be turned agayne:
But shall continue in a Godly rate,
From henceforth euermore to remayne.

Faythfull. ¶ God graunt that so it may be kept,
As all Christians it may become:
And for my part it shall not be slept,
But my duty shall straight way be done. he turneth the titles

Christian. ¶ Now God be praysed who thus agayne,
Hath restored me to my former estate:
And hath extinguished from me all payne,
God graunt that now I be not founde vngrate.
And God graunt that all Christians may me duly imbrase,
In such sorte as Gods will it is:
So shall they be sure of a resting place,
In Heauen where raigneth all ioy and blisse.

FINIS.